Southern Living® Cookbook Library

The Low Cost Cookbook

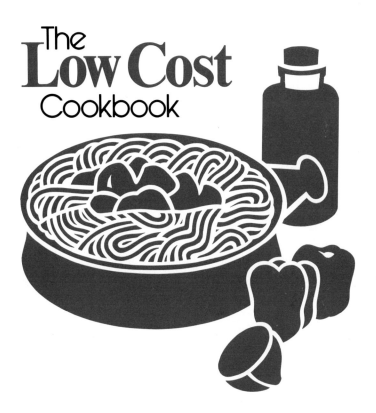

Copyright© 1972 Oxmoor House, Inc.
All rights reserved.
Library of Congress Catalog Number: 76-42146
ISBN: 0-8487-0348-0

Cover: French Fish Soup (page 40)
Left: Spanish Steak (page 50)
    Quick Strawberry-Cream Parfaits (page 177)

contents

Left: Yam Betty (page 178)
Right: Spiced Louisiana Yam Pie (page 178)

preface

M y wife is a great manager!

These words, said in a proud and appreciative tone of voice, are heartwarming to every woman who hears them. And certainly an important part of being a good manager is getting the most for your food dollar. Thousands of southern women have learned the art of seasonal buying, thrifty cooking methods, and other ways to trim their food budgets without sacrificing either quality or flavor. Now, this art is yours in the *Low-Cost Cookbook.*

In these pages, you'll find detailed shopping advice . . . innovative substitutions designed specifically to stretch your food dollar . . . wonderfully creative ways to use leftovers . . . and many more buying and preparation ideas certain to save you precious food dollars.

For generations southern women have successfully met the problem of supplying their families' nutritional needs and serving appealing meals without spending more than the budget allows for food. They have hundreds of little tricks they use to prepare memorable, low-cost meals — and in this book, they share their lore with you.

As you browse through these pages, you'll find yourself becoming excited as you discover one way after another to cut down on your food costs. You'll begin to see how you can actually have money left over from your food budget. From our kitchens to yours, welcome to the wonderful world of low-cost cookery - southern style!

4

There are two secrets to successful menu planning: nutrition and appeal. You provide nutrition by selecting all the foods your family needs for proper growth and health. Appeal is a quality you add to food — eye-appeal, taste-appeal, and the appetizing aromas which emanate from your kitchen.

NUTRITION

Beginning in the early years of this century, scientists learned that certain foods were vital to proper growth and regulation of bodily functions. As the years passed, vitamins and important minerals were identified, and their roles in sustaining life became understood. Today the foods which supply these

HIGH-QUALITY, LOW-COST

meal planning

needed vitamins and minerals are grouped into four major categories and constitute the basis for menu planning. By including recommended quantities of foods from each of these four groups, homemakers can be certain of providing the nutrients their families need.

Milk and milk products include milk (whole, reconstituted dry, or evaporated, skim, and buttermilk), cheese (cottage, cream, Cheddar and a host of other popular cheeses), cream, and ice cream. These foods provide calcium and other nutrients which build and repair bones and teeth. Recommended daily servings (an eight-ounce cup is a serving) of milk are three or more for children, four or more for teenagers, two or more for adults, and four to six for pregnant women and nursing mothers. Thrifty milk products may be substituted for milk: an eight-ounce serving of milk is equivalent to one pound of cottage cheese, three-quarters pound of cream cheese, one pint of ice cream, or one and one-third ounces of Cheddar or other type cheese.

Meat, poultry, and fish make up the second important food group. These foods supply the protein needed for normal growth, renewal of body tissues, and regulation of some bodily functions. Two or more two- to three-ounce servings of lean fish, meat, or poultry are recommended daily. Inexpensive variety meats — heart, liver, and kidney — as well as assorted luncheon meats are excellent sources of this needed protein. Or you may want to serve equally inexpensive substitutes: two eggs; one cup dried peas, beans, or lentils; or four tablespoons of peanut butter are the nutritional equivalents of one meat, fish, or poultry serving.

Fruits and vegetables are featured in the third food category. Dark green and deep yellow vegetables — like low-priced greens, spinach, kale, carrots, and squashes — are sources of Vitamin A. This vitamin is essential to the growth of young people and for the maintenance of clear skin and proper vision.

The familiar citrus fruits — also good buys in season — and some light green vegetables like celery, lettuce, and peas are sources of Vitamin C. Relatively large daily amounts of Vitamin C are required for good skin tissues and the prevention of vitamin deficiency diseases. Unlike many nutrients, Vitamin C cannot be stored in the body and must be replenished daily. Four or more servings of fruits and vegetables are recommended. One serving consists of half a cup of vegetables or fruit; or one medium apple, banana, orange, or potato; or half a medium grapefruit or melon.

The fourth important food group includes *miscellaneous foods* such as butter, margarine, fat, oil, and sugar. These foods — especially sugar — are sources of quick, high energy but should be consumed in moderation. Generally speaking, American families tend to eat too many of these foods. Cutting down on your family's intake of sugars and fats will help reduce your grocery bill while achieving a balanced diet.

APPEAL

Cutting down on wasted food is another simple way to save food dollars. And creating appealing meals is one way to ensure that every plate you serve will be cleaned. Plan meals which provide color, texture, and flavor contrast. If your main dish is pork, poultry, or fish, add color notes with deep green or bright yellow vegetables — inexpensive mixed vegetables would also be a welcome addition. Or, if green peas are on your menu, include mashed potatoes rather than the small boiled ones which are similar in shape to peas.

Mix mild and piquant flavors, soft and firm foods, and hot and cold dishes. But do consider the season. In cold weather, your family will need more hot foods, fats, and carbohydrates to help maintain body temperature. In the heat of midsummer, cold salads and iced desserts will be particularly appreciated.

Whatever the season, serve hot foods *hot* and cold foods *cold.* Warm dinner plates and refrigerator-chill salad bowls and sherbet glasses. These are thoughtful, family-pleasing gestures which make a difference in both food flavor and mealtime enjoyment.

Finally, serve appetizingly small and tidy food portions as soon as possible after preparation. Small children especially are intimidated by large amounts of food heaped on their plates. Make it a practice to serve small portions and wait for people to request seconds if they are still hungry. You'll have far less wasted food if you do!

In the sections that follow, you'll find tips about saving money at the grocery store and facts to help you buy fruits, vegetables, and meats in their seasons. Use these guides to help you plan low-cost, high quality meals for your family — and ease your food budget at the same time!

Every week, it seems, you spend more money at the local grocery store. With your big investment in food, of course you are concerned about getting the most from every grocery dollar. Wise homemakers know that there are ways to trim your food budget without sacrificing quality or flavor. Some of their most effective ideas follow:

Read the food ads. One day each week, all the grocery stores in your area will advertise their specials. In most communities, these ads appear on Wednesday or Thursday. Take the time to sit down with a heavy marking pencil or crayon and circle the first and second best buys each store is featuring. List these buys so you can easily see your greatest values.

Plan your week's menus. Using the foods that are on special sale as a foun-

shopper's guide

dation, plan your family's menus for an entire week. Don't forget to include such often-forgotten items as school lunches (if your children take lunch boxes) and after-school snacks. You'll want to feature dishes which use the specials of the week, but you'll also want to take advantage of foods in season. In the next section you'll find a calendar showing the months when various fruits, vegetables, and meats are most plentiful.

Make a detailed shopping list. Start by listing all the foods you will need to prepare the dishes you have planned for your week's menus. Then check your storage cupboards and refrigerator to see what items are running low. Here's a quick trick to cut down the time it usually takes to make a list. If you use an item during food preparation and notice that you are running low, mark the container with a grease pencil or magic marker: When you are making up your week's grocery list, all you have to do is write down the items in these marked containers — no more shaking boxes and examining the levels in your bottles.

Eat before you shop. Repeated surveys have indicated that if you are hungry when you shop for food, you may spend six or seven dollars more than if you had shopped after eating. Something about combining all that food in the store with your gnawing hunger leads you to buy more than you intended . . . or needed.

Compare prices in different stores. To get the most value for your money, you need to shop in three to five different stores for your groceries. By shopping this way, you can be certain of getting the lowest prices and of finding a large number of different items on "special." There may be some instances when it is not feasible for you personally to shop in so many stores each week — perhaps you don't have the transportation available. But generally, comparison shopping among different stores pays dividends.

Compare cost per serving. When considering fresh food, compare the *per serving* price of fresh versus both frozen and canned foods. You may actually save money buying frozen or canned vegetables or fruit, especially out of season. Consider too, the cost per serving of various cuts of meat, poultry, and fish – a normal serving is three-quarters of a pound of bone-in and one-half a pound of boneless.

Buy the store brands. A recent Federal Trade Commission survey concluded that prices of store brands average 12 percent lower than precisely the same quality of food sold under established "big brand" names.

Use your shopping list. Few things inflate a family's food bill as quickly as "impulse buying"... that insidious habit of picking up one of these and a few of those until you have added as much as one-third to your original food costs. If you really have trouble resisting the extras and keeping to a budget, invest in one of the small pocket calculators. Set a dollar amount as a limit for yourself. Punch in the price of every item you pick up, whether included on your list or not. When you reach your predetermined limit, that's it. A few times of returning those expensive extras to the shelves will cure even the most habitual impulse buyer.

Know what is a special . . . and what is not. So far, the specials we have been talking about are "loss leaders". . . items grocers feature at a loss in profit to attract customers to their stores. But there are several other specials you should know about. One is the quick markdown – a grocer may have over-stocked an item and want to clear his shelf quickly. When this happens, he usually puts up handwritten signs. These signs are often guideposts to great bargains. Another kind of special is the "rain check." If a store is out of the bargain it advertised, ask for a "rain check." This is a certificate entitling you to buy an advertised special at sale price when the item is restocked – even though it may then be marked to sell at a higher price.

Know what you are buying. Take the time to learn what the various gradings of meat, vegetables, and fruits mean. For instance, Grade A vegetables and fruits are the extra-fancy quality food usually used in fine restaurants or in dishes where the appearance of the food is important. Grade B is food intended for general consumption, and Grade C is less fancy food (it may be cut in irregular pieces, for instance) but contains the same nutrients as foods labeled Grades A and B. Grades B and C are priced lower than Grade A.

Finally, get to know the people you are dealing with. The store manager who knows you as one of his regular customers will sometimes tell you that an item is about to be put on special – he may even let you buy it a day early! The checker who remembers you from week to week will be especially careful to ring up your order quickly and correctly. And the stock boys will be glad to look in the back room for more cans or boxes of a depleted special when they recognize you as a regular customer. Your grocery store is one of the many places where a smile and a few nice words will pay off!

Wise homemakers know that one of the best ways to save food dollars is to buy seasonal specials. When produce crops mature, the markets are flooded with low-cost, high-quality fruits and vegetables. Similarly, big catches of fish mean savings in food dollars for thrifty shoppers. Poultry is also supplied on a cyclical basis as is lamb. Most meats other than lamb are in constant supply — growers have been able to control the birth and feeding of animals so that the supply of good meat is constant almost year-round.

The chart that follows tells you which foods are in season during which months. Consult it, and save dollars by buying seasonal specials. It should be

SAVINGS IN

seasonal buying

remembered, however, that this chart includes foods available in every region of our country. Check the grocery ads or newspaper agricultural section to be certain that the food you have chosen is native to your particular region.

	MEAT, POULTRY, & SEAFOOD	FRUITS AND VEGETABLES
January	roasters, stewing hens cod, bonito, flounder, striped bass; oysters	coconuts, cranberries, grapes, kumquats, persimmons, strawberries, tangerines artichokes, broccoli, Brussels sprouts, endive, rutabagas
February	flounder, pompano, pollock, smelt; hard clams, oysters	coconuts, cranberries, persimmons, strawberries, tangerines artichokes, asparagus, broccoli, Brussels sprouts, endive, rutabagas
March	Lamb cod, flounder, haddock, herring, king mackerel, striped bass, white perch, catfish; hard clams, Pacific oysters, scallops	coconuts, cranberries, rhubarb, strawberries, tangerines artichokes, asparagus, broccoli, Brussels sprouts, endive, rutabagas
April	Lamb cod, cusk, flounder haddock, halibut, mackerel, mullet, ocean perch, shad, smelt, striped bass, sturgeon, white perch, whiting, catfish; soft clams, scallops	coconuts, cranberries, rhubarb, strawberries, tangerines artichokes, asparagus, broccoli, endive, rutabagas

	MEAT, POULTRY, & SEAFOOD	FRUITS AND VEGETABLES
May	Lamb bluefish, cod, cusk, flounder, hake, halibut, ocean perch, pollock, smelt, snapper; crawfish, Maine lobster	black raspberries, blueberries, cantaloupes, cherries, coconut, dewberries, grapes, raspberries, rhubarb, strawberries, watermelons artichokes, asparagus, broccoli, corn, endive, kohlrabi, green onions
June	broilers, fryers bluefish, flounder, halibut, ocean perch Atlantic salmon, tuna; hard clams, snapper turtles	apricots, blackberries, black raspberries, blueberries, cantaloupes, cherries, coconuts, currants, dewberries, figs, grapes, honey balls, peaches, plums, raspberries, rhubarb, strawberries, watermelon asparagus, broccoli, corn, endive, kohlrabi, green onions
July	broilers, fryers flounder, hake, halibut, Atlantic and red salmon, whiting; abalone, hard clams, soft clams, soft crabs, shrimp	apricots, blackberries, black raspberries, blueberries, cantaloupes, cherries, currants, dewberries, figs, grapes, honey balls, peaches, plums, raspberries, rhubarb, strawberries, watermelon corn, kohlrabi, green onions, rutabagas
August	broilers, fryers flounder, mackerel, sole, silver salmon, tuna; hard and soft clams; blue, hard, and soft crabs, spiny lobsters; scallops; shrimp	apricots, blackberries, blueberries, cantaloupes, cherries, currants, figs, grapes, honey balls, peaches, plums, prunes, raspberries, rhubarb, watermelon corn, kohlrabi, green onions, pumpkins, rutabagas
September	fryers, roasters haddock, hake, pompano, silver salmon; hard crabs	cantaloupes, casabas, cherries, cranberries, dates, honey balls, peaches, plums, pomegranates, prunes, quinces, watermelon corn, kohlrabi, green onions, pumpkins, rutabagas
October	roasters, stewing hens bluefish, flounder, hake, mullet, Spanish mackerel, catfish; hard crabs, Maine and spiny lobsters, oysters, shrimp	cantaloupes, casabas, coconuts, cranberries, dates, grapes, honey balls, persimmons, pomegranates, prunes, quinces, satsumas, tangerines artichokes, broccoli, Brussels sprouts, endive, pumpkins, rutabagas
November	roasters, stewing hens, turkeys flounder, King mackerel, mullet, pollock, snapper, striped bass; Dungeness clams, oysters	coconuts, cranberries, dates, grapes, kumquats, persimmons, pomegranates, strawberries, tangerines artichokes, broccoli, Brussels sprouts, endive, pumpkins, rutabagas
December	roasters, stewing hens, turkeys bluefish, flounder, ocean perch, snapper, whiting; hard clams, hard crabs, shrimp	cantaloupes, casabas, coconuts, cranberries, dates, grapes, honey balls, peaches, persimmons, plums, pomegranates, prunes, quinces, satsumas Brussels sprouts, corn, endive, kohlrabi, pumpkins, rutabagas

11

Cola Fruit Salad (page 16); Congealed Fruit Salad (page 17); Congealed Vegetable Salad with Shrimp (page 24)

budget salads

Versatile . . . varied . . . nutritious . . . economical — these are just a few of the words which describe salads. Salads come in many forms — from small appetizer salads to huge Caesar salads that are a meal in themselves. Just about any kind of food can be turned into salads — and southern homemakers are experts at making that transformation.

These women appreciate the economical aspect of salads — the wonderful way in which just a few vegetables, fruits, or chunks of meat or fish become a family-pleasing salad. They have developed many flavorful recipes for all types of low-cost salads — and now the best of these are shared with you in the section that follows.

Pear and Lime Salad may be just what you need to lift a luncheon menu to new heights! And for that big family picnic, prepare Potato Salad Allemand and Slaw with dressing. These two all-time favorites are certain to bring you compliments galore.

Fancy salads haven't been neglected in this section, either. Hot Chicken Salad or Curried Rice Salad would be perfect for your next buffet party. They're easy to handle but bring sparkling flavor with each bite. Best of all, these salads and the others included in this section are all budget-trimmers. Using low-cost ingredients or leftovers, they give you delicious vegetable, fruit, meat, or cereal salads — at only pennies a serving!

PINEAPPLE SALAD

1 No. 2 1/2 can pineapple chunks	Juice of 2 lemons
2 tbsp. cornstarch	1/2 c. chopped nuts
2 eggs, well beaten	1/2 lb. miniature marshmallows
1 c. sugar	

Drain the pineapple and reserve 1 cup juice. Combine the cornstarch, eggs, reserved juice and sugar in a saucepan and cook until thick, stirring frequently. Add the lemon juice and cool. Add the pineapple and remaining ingredients and pour into a mold. Chill overnight.

Elizabeth L. Fox, Gustine, Texas

SUNFLOWER SALAD

1/2 c. cream-style cottage cheese	Fresh or canned peach slices
Salt to taste	Lettuce
Mayonnaise	1/2 c. seedless raisins

Mix the cottage cheese and salt with enough mayonnaise to moisten. Arrange peach slices on lettuce to resemble petals of sunflower. Place cheese mixture in a mound in center of peach slices and place raisins on cheese mixture to resemble seeds.

Mrs. Clara Seago, Prattville, Alabama

Tip for Freezing Apples
Apples, which have been dipped in lightly salted water to prevent discoloration, can be successfully stored in the freezer. Drop peeled, quartered, and sliced apples a few pieces at a time into cold, salted water. Transfer from water to freezer container and freeze immediately.

RED APPLE SALAD

1/4 tsp. salt	4 firm tart apples
1 1/2 c. sugar	1/2 c. cottage cheese
1/2 c. red cinnamon candies	1/4 c. chopped green pepper
3 c. water	Watercress

Mix the salt, sugar, candies and water in a saucepan. Place over low heat and stir until candies are dissolved. Pare and core the apples. Add to syrup in the saucepan and cover. Cook until apples are tender, turning occasionally to color evenly. Drain and chill. Mix the cottage cheese with green pepper and place in centers of the apples. Serve on watercress.

Mrs. Dorothy Patterson, Warner, Oklahoma

Molded Apple-Blue Cheese Salad (below)

MOLDED APPLE-BLUE CHEESE SALAD

1 pkg. lemon gelatin	3/4 c. sliced celery
1/4 tsp. salt	4 tbsp. broken walnuts
1 c. hot water	4 tbsp. crumbled
1 c. cold water	blue cheese
1 tbsp. sherry	Salad Greens
2 c. cubed Washington red	4 tbsp. mayonnaise
Delicious apples	

Dissolve the gelatin and salt in hot water in a bowl. Stir in the cold water and sherry. Arrange about 1/3 of the apples in a salad mold or bowl, then ladle in gelatin mixture until apples just start to float. Chill until firm. Chill remaining gelatin until syrupy. Place remaining apples in a bowl. Add the celery, walnuts and cheese and mix with 2 forks. Add mayonnaise and mix. Stir in the syrupy gelatin and pour over firm layer in mold. Chill until firm. Unmold onto a salad plate and garnish with desired greens. 6-8 servings.

APPLESAUCE SALAD

1 3-oz. package lemon gelatin	1 6-oz. bottle ginger ale
2 c. applesauce, heated	1/2 c. finely chopped pecans

Dissolve the gelatin in the applesauce. Stir in remaining ingredients and pour into a mold. Chill until firm.

Mrs. Gladys Nichols, Abilene, Texas

15

STUFFED BANANA SALAD

1/4 c. peanut butter	Lemon juice
2 tbsp. chopped raisins	Chopped salted peanuts
4 sm. bananas	Lettuce
Mayonnaise	

Mix the peanut butter with raisins. Peel the bananas and cut in half, then cut lengthwise. Fill sandwich-fashion with raisin mixture. Roll in mayonnaise thinned with lemon juice, then in peanuts. Serve on lettuce and garnish each serving with a red cherry or strawberry.

Mrs. F. D. Canaday, Walterboro, South Carolina

Low-Cost Bananas, In and Out of Season

When bananas are low in cost, you may want to store them for future use. Mash; sprinkle with ascorbic acid powder (available from any pharmacy), and freeze in measured amounts.

PEAR AND LIME SALAD

3/4 c. cottage cheese	1 3-oz. package lime gelatin
1 tsp. ginger	2 c. boiling water
12 sm. pear halves	Lettuce

Mix the cottage cheese with ginger. Fill pear centers with cheese mixture and place 2 halves together. Dissolve the gelatin in the water and chill until thickened. Pour a small amount of gelatin into 6 individual oiled molds. Place a pear in center of each mold and cover with remaining gelatin. Chill until firm. Serve on lettuce and garnish with mayonnaise.

Mrs. Wilbur Jenkins, Sadieville, Kentucky

COLA FRUIT SALAD

1 env. unflavored gelatin	1 1/2 c. cola or ginger ale
2 tbsp. sugar	1 1/2 c. mixed diced fruit (fresh
1/4 c. water	or canned)
Juice of 1 lemon	Whipped cream

Combine the gelatin and sugar in a saucepan. Add the water and lemon juice. Place over low heat, stirring constantly, until gelatin and sugar are dissolved. Remove from heat. Add the cola and chill until mixture is the consistency of unbeaten egg white. Fold in the mixed diced fruit. Turn into 6 stemmed glasses or individual molds. Chill until firm. Top with whipped cream. 6 servings.

Photograph for this recipe on page 12.

CONGEALED FRUIT SALAD

2 3-oz. packages cherry gelatin	2 c. fresh cantaloupe balls
1 c. fresh grapes, halved	1/2 c. fresh cherries

Prepare the gelatin according to package directions and chill until partially set. Add remaining ingredients and mix well. Pour into a mold and chill until firm.

Photograph for this recipe on page 12.

CONGEALED ORANGE SALAD

1 3-oz. package orange gelatin	1 sm. can evaporated milk
1 c. boiling water	1 c. mayonnaise
1 sm. can crushed pineapple	1 c. grated cheese

Dissolve the gelatin in the water in a bowl and stir in the pineapple. Chill until thickened. Pour the milk into a refrigerator tray and freeze until ice crystals form around edge of tray. Whip with electric mixer until stiff and fold into the gelatin. Fold in the mayonnaise and cheese and pour into a mold. Chill until firm.

Mrs. E. R. Bobo, Fort Payne, Alabama

Handy Citrus Flavor

Grated citrus rinds can add tang to many recipes. For convenience, grate rinds of citrus fruits, and store in tightly covered jar. Refrigerate until needed.

SPINACH SALAD

1 pkg. fresh spinach	1/2 tsp. dry mustard
Olive oil	1 tsp. Worcestershire sauce
Lemon juice	Garlic salt to taste
2 eggs, beaten	1/2 c. catsup
1 tbsp. sugar	1 pt. salad oil
1 tsp. salt	1/2 c. vinegar
1/2 tsp. paprika	2/3 c. warm water

Wash and drain the spinach and cut into strips. Sprinkle with desired amounts of olive oil and lemon juice and chill. Combine the eggs, sugar, salt, paprika, mustard, Worcestershire sauce, garlic salt and catsup. Pour in a blender container and blend for 10 seconds. Add the salad oil alternately with vinegar and blend until thickened. Add the warm water gradually and blend well. Place the spinach in a salad bowl and pour dressing over salad. Toss lightly. Garnish with tomato wedges, asparagus spears and hard-cooked egg slices, if desired.

Mrs. Al Gwinnett, Wilmington, Delaware

Raisin-Cabbage-Stuffed Tomatoes (below)

RAISIN-CABBAGE-STUFFED TOMATOES

1/4 c. California raisins	1/4 tsp. salt
1 1/2 c. shredded cabbage	4 lge. tomatoes
1/4 c. buttermilk	4 hard-cooked eggs, sliced
1 1/2 tsp. vinegar	Parsley
1 1/2 tsp. sugar	

Combine the raisins and cabbage in a bowl. Mix the buttermilk, vinegar, sugar and salt and toss with cabbage mixture. Chill. Peel the tomatoes. Remove pulp from tomatoes and drain shells upside down for several minutes in refrigerator. Fill centers with cabbage mixture. Place stuffed tomatoes on salad plates and garnish with eggs and parsley. 4 servings.

POTATO SALAD ALLEMAND

6 slices bacon, diced	1 tsp. salt
1 lge. onion, diced	Pepper to taste
1/4 c. vinegar	3 c. sliced cooked potatoes
2 tbsp. water	Minced parsley to taste
3 tbsp. sugar	

Fry the bacon in a skillet until crisp, then remove from skillet. Brown the onion in bacon drippings. Add the vinegar, water, sugar, salt and pepper and bring to a boil. Add the potatoes and parsley and heat thoroughly. Place in a bowl and sprinkle with bacon. 6 servings.

Mrs. Ralph Brakebill, Radcliff, Kentucky

BEET ASPIC RING

2 tbsp. unflavored gelatin	1 1/2 tbsp. horseradish
1/3 c. cold water	Dash of celery salt
2 c. boiling water	1/2 tsp. salt
2/3 c. sugar	1 c. finely chopped cabbage
1/2 c. lemon juice	1 c. chopped cooked beets
1 tbsp. vinegar	1 c. diced celery

Soften the gelatin in cold water in a bowl. Add the boiling water and sugar and stir until dissolved. Stir in the lemon juice, vinegar, horseradish, celery salt and salt and chill until partially set. Add remaining ingredients and mix well. Pour into a ring mold and chill until firm. Beet juice, heated, may be substituted for some of the boiling water to improve color and flavor.

Mrs. Wesley A. Brown, Roanoke, Virginia

GREEN BEAN SALAD

1 lb. fresh green beans	Pepper to taste
2 tsp. salt	Dash of cayenne pepper
1/2 c. cooking oil	Salad greens
1/2 c. lemon juice	1 hard-cooked egg yolk, riced
1 tsp. dry mustard	2 tbsp. capers

Wash the beans and snap the ends, pulling away strings. Leave beans whole. Bring 1 inch water to a boil in a large saucepan. Add the beans and 1 teaspoon salt and cook for 5 minutes. Cover and simmer for 10 minutes longer. Combine the oil, lemon juice, remaining salt, mustard, pepper and cayenne pepper. Drain the beans and place in a large bowl. Pour dressing over beans and mix lightly. Cool. Cover and marinate in refrigerator for at least 2 hours. Drain beans and arrange in bundles on salad greens. Garnish with egg yolk and capers.

Mrs. Mamie Booker, Pensacola, Florida

SLAW WITH DRESSING

1 cabbage, grated	1 c. finely chopped red
Juice of 1 lemon	peppers
5 hard-boiled eggs, mashed	1 tbsp. prepared mustard
1 c. finely chopped celery	3/4 c. mayonnaise
1 c. finely chopped green	Salt and pepper to taste
peppers	

Place the cabbage in a large bowl. Mix remaining ingredients and toss lightly with cabbage. 15 servings.

Mrs. R. M. Boyney, McComb, Mississippi

Garden-Style Coleslaw (below)

GARDEN-STYLE COLESLAW

1 1/2 c. shredded cabbage	1 tsp. salt
1 8 1/2-oz. can sweet peas, drained	1/2 c. sour cream
1/2 c. diced cucumber	1 tbsp. white wine vinegar
1/2 c. diced celery	4 tsp. sugar
1/4 c. chopped green pepper	1/4 tsp. prepared mustard
	Paprika

Combine the vegetables in a medium bowl and sprinkle with salt. Mix the sour cream, vinegar, sugar and mustard. Spoon over salad and toss lightly. Chill, then sprinkle with paprika. 4-6 servings.

FROZEN MINT SALAD

12 marshmallows	1 c. drained crushed pineapple
4 tbsp. pineapple juice	1/4 c. mayonnaise
4 drops of green food coloring	1/2 c. whipped dessert topping
4 drops of mint flavoring	

Melt the marshmallows in the pineapple juice in a double boiler. Stir in the food coloring and cool. Add the flavoring, pineapple and mayonnaise and mix well. Fold in the whipped topping and pour into individual molds. Freeze. May be removed from molds and wrapped in waxed paper. Place in plastic bag and store in freezer. 6 servings.

Mrs. F. H. Forester, Charleston, West Virginia

FROZEN BANANA SALAD

4 med. bananas, mashed	1/2 c. chopped maraschino cherries
2 tbsp. lemon juice	1/2 c. chopped nuts
1/2 c. sugar	1 1/2 c. whipped dessert topping
1/4 c. mayonnaise	Lettuce

Mix the bananas, lemon juice, sugar, mayonnaise, cherries and nuts and fold in whipped topping. Place in a freezing tray and freeze. Serve on lettuce leaves. 8 servings.

Mrs. G. C. Carter, Chattanooga, Tennessee

Splurge with Homemade Fruit Topping
For a luscious homemade topping on desserts and fruit or in fluffy fruit dressings, beat equal parts of instant nonfat dry milk and cold liquid into stiff peaks. Add lemon juice at the soft-peak stage to stabilize the whipping and highlight the flavor.

FROZEN CRANBERRY SALAD

1 16-oz. can jellied cranberry sauce	1/4 c. mayonnaise
3 tbsp. lemon juice	1/2 c. confectioners' sugar
2 c. whipped dessert topping	1/2 c. chopped nuts
	Lettuce

Mash the cranberry sauce in a bowl and stir in the lemon juice. Pour into paper cups or refrigerator tray. Combine remaining ingredients and spread over cranberry mixture. Freeze until firm. Unmold on lettuce. 8 servings.

Mrs. J. T. Teas, Haleyville, Alabama

PICADOR SALAD

1 lb. ground beef	1 tbsp. chili powder
1/4 c. chopped onion	4 c. shredded lettuce
2 c. drained kidney beans	1/2 c. sliced green onions
1/2 c. bottled French dressing	1/2 lb. sharp Cheddar cheese, shredded
1/2 c. water	

Brown the ground beef in a skillet. Add onion and cook until tender. Stir in the beans, French dressing, water and chili powder and simmer for 15 minutes. Combine the lettuce and green onions. Add the beef mixture and 1 1/2 cups cheese and toss lightly. Sprinkle with remaining cheese. Serve with crisp tortillas. 4-6 servings.

Mrs. J. B. Garner, Anderson, South Carolina

CONGEALED HAM SALAD

1 tbsp. unflavored gelatin	1/2 c. chopped celery
1/4 c. cold water	1 tbsp. minced onion
3/4 c. boiling water	1/2 c. mayonnaise
1/4 c. vinegar	1 1/4 c. ground cooked ham
1/2 tsp. salt	2 hard-cooked eggs, sliced
1/2 c. chopped pimento	

Soak the gelatin in cold water for 5 minutes, then dissolve in the boiling water. Stir in the vinegar and salt and chill until partially set. Fold in remaining ingredients except eggs. Arrange the egg slices on bottom and sides of mold and spoon gelatin mixture into mold. Chill until firm and garnish with parsley.

Mrs. Kenneth Brett, Emporia, Virginia

CORNED BEEF SALAD

1 pkg. lemon or celery gelatin	Minced onion to taste (opt.)
1 c. mayonnaise	3 hard-boiled eggs, diced
1 pkg. frozen peas, thawed	1 can corned beef, diced
1 c. diced celery	

Place gelatin in a shallow flat dish. Add 1 cup boiling water and stir until dissolved. Add 1/2 cup cold water and mix well. Chill until partially set. Stir in the remaining ingredients and chill until set. Cut into squares and serve on lettuce leaves.

Mrs. F. C. MacMichael, Holly Hill, Florida

HOT CHICKEN SALAD

2/3 c. mayonnaise or salad dressing	1 c. diced celery
2 tsp. cider vinegar	1/4 c. blanched slivered almonds
1 tsp. salt	1/4 c. chopped sweet pickles
1/4 tsp. celery seed	2 tsp. chopped onion
1/8 tsp. pepper	1 c. crushed potato chips
2 c. diced cooked chicken	

Preheat oven to 350 degrees. Mix the mayonnaise with vinegar, salt, celery seed and pepper. Combine the chicken with celery, almonds, pickles and onion and toss with mayonnaise mixture. Place in a 10 x 6 x 2-inch baking dish or individual casseroles and sprinkle with potato chips. Bake for 20 minutes. Garnish with parsley or pickle fans. One cup grated cheese may be substituted for potato chips. 6 servings.

Mrs. Robert Chapman, Uniontown, Kentucky

TURKEY-MACARONI SALAD

1 8-oz. package elbow macaroni	1/2 c. chopped green pepper
1 1/2 c. diced cooked turkey	1/4 c. pickle relish
1 c. diced celery	Mayonnaise
1 sm. onion, minced	Salt and pepper to taste

Cook the macaroni in boiling, salted water until tender and drain. Rinse in cold water and cool. Add the turkey, celery, onion, green pepper, relish and enough mayonnaise to moisten. Season with salt and pepper and mix well. Serve on salad greens, if desired. 6 servings.

Mrs. Reddick Lyons, Jacksonville, Florida

FRESH APPLE-TURKEY SALAD

2 c. diced Washington red or golden	2 tbsp. chopped chives or parsley
Delicious apples	2/3 c. mayonnaise
3 c. diced cooked turkey	1 tsp. sweet basil or salad herbs
3 tbsp. lemon juice	Salt and pepper to taste
2/3 c. diced celery	Lettuce
3 hard-cooked eggs, chopped	1 unpared Washington apple, sliced
1/2 c. chopped toasted almonds	

Combine the diced apples and turkey in a bowl and sprinkle with lemon juice. Toss lightly, then add the celery, eggs, almonds and chives. Blend the mayonnaise, basil, salt and pepper and fold into turkey mixture. Serve in lettuce cups with apple slices for garnish. 4-6 servings.

Fresh Apple-Turkey Salad (above)

HEARTY SUPPER SALAD

1 1/2 c. diced cooked turkey	3 tbsp. pickle vinegar
1 c. sliced celery	3/4 c. mayonnaise
2 hard-cooked eggs, diced	Salt and pepper to taste
4 sweet pickles, cut in strips	Grated onion to taste (opt.)

Mix all ingredients in a bowl and chill. Serve over lettuce. 4 servings.

Mrs. Jesse Melton, Erie, Tennessee

FLAKED FISH SALAD

1 c. cooked fish flakes	1/8 tsp. pepper
1 c. shredded cabbage	2 hard-cooked eggs, chopped
1/2 c. chopped celery	2 tbsp. chopped onion
2 tbsp. chopped sweet pickle	Mayonnaise or salad dressing
1/2 tsp. salt	Lettuce

Mix the fish flakes, cabbage, celery, pickle, salt, pepper, eggs and onion in a bowl and stir in enough mayonnaise to moisten. Serve on lettuce and garnish with tomato wedges and olives, if desired. 4-5 servings.

Flora T. Loftus, Miami, Florida

JELLIED TUNA SALAD

1 tbsp. unflavored gelatin	1/4 c. vinegar
1/2 tsp. salt	2 eggs, beaten
1/2 tsp. celery seed	2 c. flaked canned tuna

Sprinkle the gelatin in 1/4 cup cold water and let soak for several minutes. Add the seasonings, vinegar and 1/4 cup water to eggs. Cook over boiling water until thickened, stirring constantly, then add the gelatin and stir until dissolved. Add the tuna and mix thoroughly. Pour into individual molds or large ring mold and chill until firm. 4 servings.

Charlie Wayne Lucas, Terrell, Texas

CONGEALED VEGETABLE SALAD WITH SHRIMP

2 3-oz. packages lime gelatin	1 stalk celery
1 pkg. fresh radishes	1 1-lb. package frozen
1 lge. fresh carrot	cleaned shrimp, thawed

Prepare the gelatin according to package directions. Pour half the gelatin into a mold and chill until partially set. Chill remaining gelatin until syrupy. Wash the radishes. Remove tips and stems and chill. Slice the carrot lengthwise with a vegetable peeler and place in warm water for several minutes or until pliable. Drain. Wrap each slice around a knife handle and secure with a toothpick. Place in a bowl of cold water. Cut the celery into 2-inch lengths, then slice each length several times about halfway down. Place in the cold water with carrot curls and chill for about 30 minutes. Drain and remove toothpicks. Add the radishes and carrot curls to gelatin in the mold and mix carefully to keep carrot curls intact. Place the celery fans in the gelatin mixture. Pour syrupy gelatin into the mold and chill until firm. Unmold and place on a serving plate. Garnish with shrimp.

Photograph for this recipe on page 12.

DELUXE SALMON MOLD

1 can red salmon	1 c. chopped celery
1 can tomato soup	1 green pepper, chopped
1/2 lb. cheese, grated	1 sm. onion, chopped
2 tbsp. unflavored gelatin	1 tbsp. catsup
3 tbsp. lemon juice	1 c. mayonnaise

Drain the salmon and remove skin and bones, then flake. Heat the soup and add the cheese, then stir until melted. Soften the gelatin in 1/2 cup cold water and add to the soup mixture, stirring until dissolved. Combine all the ingredients and pour into a mold. Chill overnight. 10-12 servings.

Mrs. Kent Rogers, Moore, Oklahoma

COLORFUL COTTAGE SALAD

1 3-oz. package lemon gelatin	1 c. cream-style cottage cheese
1 c. hot water	1/2 c. salad dressing
1/2 green pepper, minced	1/2 tsp. salt
1/2 tsp. grated onion	1/2 tsp. sugar
1 c. diced celery	1/4 c. chopped pimento

Dissolve the gelatin in hot water. Add remaining ingredients and mix well. Pour into a mold. Chill until firm and serve on lettuce.

Mrs. Lillian Herman, Bay City, Texas

PINK CREAM CHEESE SALAD

1 env. unflavored gelatin	1 3-oz. package cream cheese, softened
1/4 c. cold water	2 tsp. minced onion
1 1/2 c. tomato juice, heated	1/2 c. mayonnaise
1/4 tsp. salt	

Soften the gelatin in cold water. Add to tomato juice and stir until gelatin is dissolved. Mix the salt, cream cheese, and onion. Blend in tomato juice mixture gradually and chill until consistency of unbeaten egg white. Fold in the mayonnaise and pour into a mold or 4 individual molds. Chill until set.

Mrs. Earl Faulkenberry, Lancaster, South Carolina

HERBED COTTAGE CHEESE-VEGETABLE SALAD

1 pt. cottage cheese	1 tbsp. chopped chives
1/4 c. grated carrots	1 tbsp. chopped parsley
1/4 c. chopped celery	Pepper to taste
1/4 c. chopped green pepper	Lettuce leaves
1/2 tsp. salt	8 tomato slices
1/8 tsp. basil	

Mix all ingredients well except lettuce and tomatoes in a bowl and cover. Refrigerate for several hours to blend flavors. Place slice of tomato on lettuce leaf for each serving and mound cheese mixture on top.

Mrs. C. R. Herman, Hickory, North Carolina

EGG CURRY RING

1 1/2 tbsp. unflavored gelatin	1 1/2 c. mayonnaise
1/4 c. cold water	3 hard-cooked eggs, chopped
2 c. chicken broth	6 stuffed olives, chopped (opt.)
1 tbsp. curry powder	1/2 tsp. salt

Soften the gelatin in cold water. Bring broth to a boil in a saucepan and add the curry powder. Add the gelatin and stir until dissolved. Chill until thickened. Blend in mayonnaise and fold in the eggs, olives and salt. Pour into a ring mold rinsed with cold water and chill until firm.

Mrs. Charles F. Hunter, New Orleans, Louisiana

NOODLE-CARROT SALAD

1 sm. package noodles	2 stalks celery, chopped
1 lge. green pepper, chopped	4 sm. green onions, sliced
4 sm. carrots, grated	1/2 tsp. salt
2 tbsp. chopped pimento	Mayonnaise or salad dressing

Cook the noodles according to package directions. Drain and cool. Stir in remaining ingredients, adding enough mayonnaise to moisten. Chill.

Mrs. T. W. Taylor, Abbeville, South Carolina

SALAD SUPREME

1 c. elbow or shell macaroni	6 tbsp. chopped green pepper
1 c. chopped celery	1 c. diced sharp cheese
6 tbsp. chopped sweet pickle	1/2 c. cooked green peas
3 tbsp. chopped pimento	1/2 c. salad dressing

Cook the macaroni according to package directions, then drain. Chill for 2 hours. Add the celery, pickle, pimento, green pepper, cheese, peas and salad dressing and toss lightly. Chill. 6 servings.

Mary Nan Fitch, Electra, Texas

CURRIED RICE SALAD

1 1/2 c. cooked rice	2 tsp. salt
1/4 c. minced onion	1 c. chopped celery
1 tbsp. vinegar	1 c. cooked green peas
2 tbsp. salad oil	1/2 c. salad dressing or
1 tsp. curry powder	mayonnaise

Combine the rice, onion, vinegar, salad oil, curry powder and salt in a bowl and chill for several hours. Add remaining ingredients and mix well. 4-6 servings.

Mrs. John R. Snow, Fort Monroe, Virginia

PATIO NOODLE SALAD

4 c. cooked noodles, chilled	2 tsp. prepared mustard
1 c. sour cream	2 c. sliced celery
1/2 c. salad dressing or	3/4 c. sliced radishes
mayonnaise	1 c. cubed Cheddar cheese
1/4 c. sliced green onion	1/2 lb. sliced bologna or cotto
2 tsp. seasoned salt	salami, diced

Combine the noodles, sour cream, salad dressing, green onion, salt and mustard in a bowl and chill for about 1 hour to blend flavors. Add remaining ingredients and mix. Store in refrigerator until ready to serve. 8-10 servings.

Patio Noodle Salad (above)

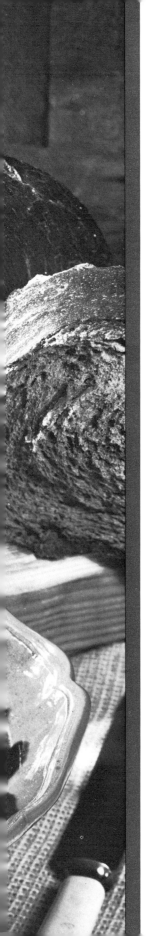

Spanish Beef Stew with Olives (page 30)

thrifty soups and stews

Bubbling pots of appetite-arousing liquids . . . bright vegetables in a shimmering broth . . . great chunks of meat cooked to the point of flavorful perfection — this is the wonderful world of soups and stews.

It *is* a wonderful world, not only for flavor and nutritional values, but for economy. Generations of thrifty southern homemakers have cooked bits of meat, chunks of leftover vegetables, and bones from their fine roasts to create unforgettable soups and stews. That's how the classic southern soup known as gumbo originated.

In the pages that follow, you'll find recipes for gumbo and many other soups and stews developed by southern homemakers in their own kitchens . . . for their own families. Beef Stew Viennese and Ranch-style Stew are two hearty and filling beef dishes sure to bring requests for more. Poultry is featured, too, in such recipes as Chicken Stew and Dumplings. These are just some of the dishes awaiting you — turn these pages and discover many, many more.

Every recipe you'll find is the proud creation of the *Southern Living* homemaker who now shares it with you. Why not plan to serve your appreciative family a sustaining and flavorful soup or stew at your next meal — from one of the home-perfected, low-cost recipes awaiting you in this section!

APPLESAUCE-BEEF STEW

3 lb. boneless beef	1/2 tsp. chili powder
Seasoned flour	5 c. boiling water
3 tbsp. shortening	2 c. applesauce
1/2 tsp. pepper	6 med. potatoes, cut in half
1 c. diced celery	6 med. onions
1 bay leaf	6 med. carrots, halved
1 8-oz. can tomato sauce	

Cut the beef in 1-inch cubes and dredge with seasoned flour. Brown in shortening in a saucepan. Add remaining ingredients except potatoes, onions and carrots and bring to boiling point. Simmer, covered, for about 2 hours or until beef is tender. Add the vegetables and simmer for 30 minutes or until vegetables are tender. May be thickened with 1 tablespoon flour mixed with 1 tablespoon cool water. 6-8 servings.

Mrs. Jewell Dunning, Boaz, Kentucky

BEEF-LENTIL SOUP

1 1/2 to 2 lb. soup beef	1 med. potato, diced
2 quarts cold water	1 onion, diced
1 1/2 c. lentils	2 stalks celery, diced
1 carrot, diced	Salt to taste

Place the soup beef and water in a 3-quart kettle and bring to a boil. Skim carefully. Add remaining ingredients and cook over low heat for 1 hour and 30 minutes or until beef is tender. Garnish with parsley.

Kathrine F. Shinn, Mocksville, North Carolina

SPANISH BEEF STEW WITH OLIVES

2 tbsp. olive or salad oil	4 peeled tomatoes, quartered
3 1/2 lb. beef stew meat, cubed	1 bay leaf
1 tsp. salt	4 parsley sprigs
1/8 tsp. pepper	1/2 tsp. thyme leaves
2 med. onions, sliced	1 1/2 c. pimento-stuffed olives
2 lge. cloves of garlic, crushed	2 1/2 lb. peeled potatoes, halved
2 c. beef bouillon	2 tbsp. flour
2 c. dry red wine or additional bouillon	Parsley (opt.)

Heat the oil in a large kettle or Dutch oven. Add the stew meat, small amount at a time, and brown well on all sides. Remove stew meat and season with salt and pepper. Add onions to oil remaining in kettle and cook until lightly browned. Add the garlic, bouillon, wine and 1 tomato. Tie the bay leaf, parsley and thyme in cheesecloth and add to the onion mixture. Add the stew meat and bring to a boil. Cover and simmer for 2 hours or until stew meat is tender. Add the olives and potatoes and cook for 30 minutes longer. Remove stew meat and vegetables to a serving dish and keep warm. Drain cooking liquid into a saucepan and skim off fat. Bring to a boil. Blend the flour with 3 tablespoons water and stir into boiling liquid. Add remaining tomatoes and simmer for 10 minutes. Pour liquid over meat and vegetables and top with tomatoes. Garnish with parsley. Stew may be cooled before adding olives and potatoes, then frozen. Thaw over very low heat and bring to a boil before adding remaining ingredients. Stew may be baked in 350-degree oven instead of simmered. 8-10 servings.

Photograph for this recipe on page 28.

IRISH STEW

2 lb. beef	6 to 8 potatoes, quartered
1 1-lb. 3-oz. can tomatoes	3 or 4 carrots, thickly sliced
2 c. stock	2 stalks celery, sliced
1 tsp. salt	2 tbsp. cornstarch
1/4 tsp. pepper	1/4 c. cold water
6 to 8 white onions	

Cut the beef into 1 1/2-inch cubes and place in a large kettle. Add the tomatoes, stock, salt and pepper and cover. Simmer for about 45 minutes or until beef is almost tender. Add the vegetables and simmer for 45 minutes or until beef and vegetables are fork tender. Blend the cornstarch and water and add to stew gradually, stirring carefully so vegetables are not crushed. Cook over medium heat, stirring constantly, until mixture thickens and comes to a boil. Season with additional salt and pepper, if needed. Simmer for several minutes longer to blend flavors. Stew improves on standing and may be prepared ahead of time. 6-8 servings.

Irish Stew (above)

BEEF STEW VIENNESE

1/4 c. melted butter	Flour
4 onions, chopped	1 pt. meat stock
4 carrots, chopped	1 c. brown bread crumbs
2 turnips, chopped	Pinch of mace
4 lb. lean beef, cut in cubes	1 1/2 pt. white wine
Salt and pepper to taste	

Pour the butter into a large casserole and spread over sides. Place the onions, carrots and turnips in the butter. Season the beef with salt and pepper and dredge with flour. Place over vegetables and cover. Bake at 350 degrees for one hour, basting occasionally. Pour off excess fat and add the meat stock. Bake until the beef is tender. Stir in the bread crumbs and mace, then stir in the white wine. Serve with potatoes. 8 servings.

Mrs. Henry Hamilton, Morton, Mississippi

Homemade Beef Bouillon Cubes
Collect and freeze beef bones until you have 1 1/2 to 2 pounds. In a soup kettle, barely cover bones with water and simmer. After broth is hearty and seasoned, pour the concentrate into ice cube trays. Store the frozen broth cubes in plastic bags.

CHIPPED BEEF CHOWDER

1/2 c. chopped onion	1 c. milk
1 pkg. chipped beef, chopped	2 tbsp. flour
2 tbsp. butter or margarine	1 can corn
1 c. water	1 tsp. parsley flakes
2 c. diced potatoes	Salt and pepper to taste
1 c. diced carrots	

Cook the onion and chipped beef in butter in a saucepan until the onion is tender. Add the water, potatoes and carrots and cover. Simmer until the carrots are tender. Blend small amount of milk with the flour. Stir in remaining milk, then stir into potato mixture. Add the corn and parsley and bring to a boil. Season with salt and pepper.

Mrs. Edgar Neilson, Miami, Florida

CORNED BEEF STEW

1 sm. onion, chopped	1/2 c. cooked rice
1/2 c. sliced okra	1 can corned beef hash
1 c. diced tomatoes	Bacon drippings to taste
2 beef bouillon cubes	Salt and pepper to taste

Cook the onion, okra, 2 cups water, tomatoes and bouillon cubes in a saucepan until tomatoes are tender. Add the rice, corned beef hash, bacon drippings, salt and pepper and cook until flavors are blended.

Mrs. Bill Morrison, Alexander City, Alabama

> **Cut Your Own Stew Meat**
> Instead of buying pre-cut beef stew meat, buy an oversized chuck roast. Whatever meat is not needed for immediate use can be cut into beef chunks and frozen. Chuck meat on sale is less costly than pre-cut stew meat.

OVEN STEW

1 1/2 lb. lean beef	1/2 tsp. peppercorns
Beef drippings or suet	2 c. hot water
1 onion, sliced	2 c. canned tomatoes
1 carrot, sliced	3 tbsp. butter or margarine
2 sprigs of parsley	3 tbsp. flour
1 1/2 tsp. salt	1 c. cooked peas

Cut the beef in 1 1/2-inch cubes and brown in small amount of drippings in a skillet. Place in a baking dish. Add the onion, carrot, parsley, salt, peppercorns, water and tomatoes and cover. Bake at 250 degrees for 3 hours. Mix the butter and flour and stir into the stew. Bake for 30 minutes longer. Stir in the peas and remove the peppercorns. 6 servings.

Mary Nelle Hardy, Memphis, Tennessee

SPRING DILL SOUP

1 lb. stewing veal	5 med. potatoes, diced
1 sm. onion, chopped	1 med. bunch dill tops
2 tbsp. butter	Salt to taste
2 qt. water	Pinch of saffron

Cut the stew veal into 1-inch cubes. Cook the veal and onion in butter in a large saucepan until light brown. Add the water and bring to a boil. Simmer until tender. Add the remaining ingredients and simmer until potatoes are done. 6 servings.

Mrs. Russell Carter, Montgomery, Alabama

SUCCULENT VEAL STEW

2 lge. potatoes	1 lb. veal, cubed
2 lge. onions	1 tsp. salt
1 bell pepper	1/2 tsp. pepper
3 carrots	4 tbsp. Worcestershire sauce
1 or 2 stalks celery	1/2 c. water

Peel the potatoes and cut in medium pieces. Quarter the onions. Cut the bell pepper, carrots and celery in medium pieces. Place vegetables and the veal in deep, foil-lined baking pan. Add the seasonings and water and fold and seal the foil. Bake for 2 hours in 350-degree oven. 4 servings.

Mrs. Betty Wilson, Monroe, Louisiana

BEEF SOUP

2 lb. ground beef	3 c. diced celery
1 stick margarine	1 lge. can tomatoes
4 qt. water	1/2 c. pearl barley
1 c. diced carrots	2 tsp. salt
2 c. diced onions	3 tsp. pepper

Brown the beef in margarine in a heavy kettle then add the water, carrots, onions, celery, tomatoes, barley, salt and pepper. Simmer for 2 hours, stirring occasionally. Serve with crackers.

Mrs. Lillian Herman, Bay City, Texas

CABBAGE PATCH STEW

1 lb. hamburger	1 tsp. chili powder
1 med. onion, chopped	1/2 tsp. pepper
1/2 c. sliced celery	1 can kidney beans
1/2 c. chopped green pepper	1 can tomatoes
1 tsp. salt	3 c. shredded cabbage

Combine the hamburger, onion, celery and green pepper in a kettle and cook, stirring, until hamburger is partially done. Add remaining ingredients and bring to a boil. Reduce heat and simmer for 20 minutes.

Mrs. Paul D. Spradlin, Russellville, Arkansas

Frozen Chili

A practical way to store portioned quantities of chili is in ice cube trays. Freeze chili in trays; transfer cubes to plastic bags for storage. Thaw needed number of cubes; heat in saucepan.

CHILI BEANS

3 c. pinto beans	1 1/2 tbsp. chili powder
1 slice bacon	1 tsp. pepper
2 lb. ground beef	1 tsp. salt
1 garlic clove, minced	1 can tomato sauce
1 med. onion, chopped	1/2 c. catsup
Pinch of comino seed	2 tbsp. prepared mustard

Place the beans in a saucepan and cover with water. Add the bacon and bring to a boil. Reduce heat and simmer until beans are almost done. Brown the ground beef in a skillet, then stir into the beans. Add remaining ingredients and cook until beef is tender and most of the liquid has evaporated.

Mrs. Ardy Blakley, Rosebud, Texas

MEATBALL SOUP

1 lb. ground beef	2 tsp. salt
1/2 c. soft bread crumbs	2 qt. water
2 tsp. milk	2 8-oz. cans tomato sauce
2 tsp. instant minced onion	2 beef bouillon cubes
1/4 tsp. pepper	1 tsp. savory
1/2 tsp. garlic salt	1/4 c. alphabet macaroni or fine
1 tsp. Worcestershire sauce	noodles

Combine the ground beef with bread crumbs, milk, onion, pepper, garlic salt, Worcestershire sauce and 1 teaspoon salt and shape into balls about 1 inch in diameter. Add remaining salt to water in a saucepan and bring to a boil. Add the meatballs and remaining ingredients and simmer for 30 minutes. 6 servings.

Margie Fay Parker, Bradford, Tennessee

Thrifty Homemade Soup

Liquid from meats and canned vegetables, to which morsels of leftovers are added, can be frozen in a plastic container for future use. When thawed, add meat, vegetables, or noodles to make a nutritious, flavorful soup or stew.

RANCH-STYLE STEW

1 lb. ground beef	1 No. 2 can kidney beans
1 med. onion, diced	1 tsp. salt
1 green pepper, diced	2 c. tomatoes
1 tbsp. shortening	1 tsp. chili powder
1 1/2 c. whole kernel corn	1/2 c. water

Brown the beef, onion and green pepper in shortening in a large saucepan. Add the corn, beans, salt, tomatoes, chili powder and water and simmer for 20 minutes.

June Windsor, Marlow, Oklahoma

TASTY CHILI

1 lb. ground beef	1 tbsp. Worcestershire sauce
1 tbsp. bacon drippings	1 tsp. salt
2 sm. onions, chopped	2 tsp. chili powder
1 No. 2 1/2 can tomatoes	1/8 tsp. cayenne pepper
1 No. 2 can kidney beans	1/4 tsp. garlic powder
2 tbsp. chopped green pepper	

Brown the beef in drippings in a saucepan. Add the onions, tomatoes, beans, green pepper and seasonings and cook over low heat for about 1 hour, adding water, if needed. 4-6 servings.

Mrs. Lamar Vasser, Cornelia, Georgia

INDIAN CORN STEW

1 med. onion, chopped
1/3 c. chopped green pepper
2 tbsp. margarine
1 lb. ground beef
2 1/2 c. cut fresh corn

1 11-oz. can tomato soup
2 tsp. sugar
1 1/2 tsp. salt
1 tbsp. Worcestershire sauce

Cook the onion and green pepper in margarine in a saucepan until tender. Add the beef and brown well. Add corn, tomato soup, sugar, salt and Worcestershire sauce and simmer for 1 hour.

Mrs. Norman Milam, Bowling Green, Kentucky

Recycling Milk Cartons
Pour soup into well-rinsed, empty milk cartons; freeze. To remove, run warm water over carton until soup thaws around edges. Slice soup block from carton into saucepan.

SATURDAY NIGHT SOUP

1 env. onion soup mix
1 1-lb. can meatballs with
   gravy

1 1-lb. can cream-style corn
1 can tomato soup

Prepare the onion soup according to package directions. Add remaining ingredients and heat through. 6-8 servings.

Mrs. Jesse I. Strouss, Collinsville, Alabama

HAM RAGOUT

2 c. cubed cooked ham
2 tbsp. chopped onion
Margarine
2 c. cubed cooked potatoes
1 c. diced cooked celery
1 c. sliced cooked carrots

2 tbsp. chopped green pepper
2 tbsp. flour
2 c. milk
1 tsp. salt
Dash of pepper

Brown the ham and onion in 1/4 cup margarine. Add the potatoes, celery, carrots and green pepper and mix well. Place in a greased 1 1/2-quart casserole. Melt 3 tablespoons margarine in a saucepan and stir in flour. Add the milk and seasonings and cook over low heat until thickened, stirring constantly. Pour over ham mixture. Bake at 375 degrees for 30 minutes. 6 servings.

Mrs. H. B. Litchfield, Jacksonville, Florida

WHITE BEAN SOUP

2 c. dried navy beans	3 onions, finely chopped
3 qt. water	1 stalk celery, chopped
1 hambone with meat	1 clove of garlic, minced
1/2 c. cooked mashed potatoes	1/4 c. finely chopped parsley

Place the beans in a kettle, cover with water and soak overnight. Add the hambone and cover beans with water. Simmer for 1 hour. Add the potatoes and stir until well mixed. Add the onions, celery, garlic and parsley and simmer for 1 hour, stirring occasionally. Remove hambone from soup, cut off meat and place in soup.

Mrs. Lillian Herman, Bay City, Texas

SOUP MACEDOINE

2 tbsp. butter	1 c. boiling water
1/2 c. finely chopped onion	2 c. diced cooked ham
2 c. small potato cubes	1 qt. milk
1 c. thinly sliced carrots	Salt and pepper to taste
2 c. sliced green beans	Finely minced parsley

Melt the butter in a heavy saucepan or kettle. Add the onion and cook until transparent but not brown. Add the potato cubes, carrots, green beans and water. Bring to a boil and cover. Cook for 25 to 30 minutes or until vegetables are tender, adding water, if necessary. Mash the vegetables, leaving some small pieces for texture. Add the ham and milk and heat to serving temperature. Season. Serve at once with a topping of parsley. Asparagus, diced cauliflower or turnips may be substituted for green beans. 6-8 servings.

Soup Macedoine (above)

CHICKEN SOUP

1 fryer, disjointed	1 No. 303 can tomatoes
1 sm. onion, chopped	3 carrots, sliced
Chopped celery to taste	6 potatoes, chopped
Salt to taste	1 No. 303 can cream-style corn
1 med. chili pod	

Place the fryer, onion, celery and salt in large saucepan and cover with water. Cook until fryer is tender, adding water, if necessary. Add the chili pod, tomatoes, carrots and potatoes and cook until vegetables are tender. Add the corn and bring to a boil. Remove from heat. Remove the chili pod and discard.

Mrs. LeRoy Alms, Houston, Texas

GROUNDNUT STEW

1 chicken, disjointed	2 bottled red chili peppers
2 c. water	Salt to taste
2 onions, sliced	1 c. ground roasted peanuts

Place the chicken, water, onions, chili peppers, salt and peanuts in a saucepan and bring to a boil. Reduce heat and simmer for about 2 hours or until thick. Serve over rice and garnish with orange slices. 4 servings.

Mrs. Gary Parnell, Dothan, Alabama

Resourceful Poultry Planning

When disjointing and trimming poultry, reserve and freeze enough wing tips, drumstick ends, necks, tails, and giblets for a large kettle of soup. After simmering, the stewed chicken pieces may be used in creamed recipes; chicken soup may be prepared from the stock and frozen in meal-sized containers. You need only thaw and heat the soup before serving.

CHICKEN STEW AND DUMPLINGS

1 3-lb. chicken, disjointed	1/4 tsp. poultry seasoning
1 tsp. salt	1 can cream of chicken soup
1/4 tsp. paprika	2 10-oz. packages frozen mixed
Dash of pepper	vegetables
2 tbsp. butter or margarine	1 10-count pkg. refrigerator
1 c. sliced onions	biscuits

Sprinkle the chicken with salt, paprika and pepper. Melt the butter in a large skillet. Add the chicken and cook until brown on all sides. Add 1 cup water, onions and poultry seasoning and mix well. Cover. Simmer for 30 minutes. Add the soup, 1 soup can water and mixed vegetables and stir until well blended. Cover and simmer for 30 minutes. Place biscuits on top and cover. Cook for 10 minutes. Remove cover and cook for 10 minutes longer. 4-6 servings.

Doris Brim, Stoneville, North Carolina

Turkey Soup Royale (below)

TURKEY SOUP ROYALE

1/4 c. butter	1 c. Turkey Stock
1/4 c. flour	3 hard-cooked eggs, finely chopped
1 tsp. salt	1 10-oz. package frozen peas
1/8 tsp. pepper	and carrots, cooked
3 c. milk	1 c. chopped cooked turkey

Melt the butter in a 3-quart saucepan and stir in the flour, salt and pepper. Remove from heat and stir in milk and Turkey Stock gradually. Cook over medium heat, stirring constantly, until thickened, then cook for 2 minutes longer. Stir in the eggs, peas and carrots and turkey and heat to serving temperature. Serve immediately. 6 1/2 cups.

Turkey Stock

1 3-lb. turkey carcass and meat	1 med. carrot, chopped
6 c. water	1 sm. bay leaf, crushed
1 stalk celery with leaves,	1 tsp. salt
chopped	2 whole cloves
1 sm. onion, chopped	1/4 tsp. pepper

Break up the turkey carcass and place in a large kettle. Add the water, celery, onion, carrot, bay leaf, salt, cloves and pepper and cover. Bring to a boil. Reduce heat and simmer for 3 to 4 hours, turning bones occasionally. Strain. Remove meat from bones and add to stock. Add sufficient water, if necessary, to make 4 cups liquid and chill. Remove fat from top, then freeze in 1-cup portions. 4 cups.

CREAMY SHRIMP GUMBO

1 can cream of chicken soup	1/2 c. chopped shrimp, cooked
1 soup can milk	1/4 tsp. soy sauce
1 can chicken gumbo	Dash of garlic powder

Blend the cream of chicken soup and milk in a saucepan, then stir in remaining ingredients. Heat through but do not boil. 4-6 servings.

Shirleen Gammon, Glasgow, Kentucky

FRENCH FISH SOUP

1 onion, chopped	1 1-lb. package cod fillets
1 clove of garlic, crushed	1 tsp. salt
2 tbsp. chopped parsley	Dash of white pepper
1 tsp. saffron	Cayenne pepper to taste
2 tbsp. oil	Dash of thyme
1 can tomatoes	1 bay leaf
1 beef bouillon cube	1 4-oz. can mussels
1 1-lb. package flounder	1 sm. can shrimp, drained
fillets	Juice of 1 lemon

Brown the onion, garlic, parsley and saffron in the oil in a kettle. Add the tomatoes and liquid and crush tomatoes. Mix well. Add the bouillon. Cut the flounder and cod in small pieces and add to the tomato mixture. Add the salt, white pepper, cayenne pepper, thyme and bay leaf and cover. Simmer for about 12 minutes. Add the mussels with liquid and the shrimp and simmer for 10 minutes longer. Add the lemon juice and garnish with additional parsley. 6 servings.

Photograph for this recipe on cover.

SALMON STEW

1 qt. milk	1 can pink salmon
1/4 lb. margarine	Salt and pepper to taste

Scald the milk in a saucepan and add margarine. Remove bones from the salmon and mash the salmon. Stir into milk mixture and season with salt and pepper. Bring to a boil and remove from heat.

Mrs. Wilma Harrison, Donalsonville, Georgia

CATFISH STEW

12 sm. catfish	1 16-oz. can cream-style corn
6 qt. water	2 8-oz. cans tomato paste
3 slices salt pork, diced	1 lge. can evaporated milk
4 1/2 c. cubed potatoes	Salt and pepper to taste
3 c. diced onions	

Place the catfish and water in a kettle and bring to a boil. Reduce heat and simmer until catfish are tender. Remove catfish from water and cool. Remove fish from bones and place fish back in broth. Fry the salt pork in a skillet until brown and remove from skillet. Add drippings to broth. Add remaining ingredients except milk, salt and pepper and simmer until potatoes are tender. Remove from heat and stir in the milk, salt and pepper.

Mrs. Cordelia Webb, Greenville, South Carolina

BOUILLABAISSE A L'AMERICAINE

1/2 c. salad oil	1 1/2 tsp. salt
1 lge. onion, chopped	3 c. water
1 clove of garlic, minced	2 lb. fresh or frozen fish fillets
1 1-lb. can tomatoes	1 frozen lobster, thawed
3 strips California lemon peel	1/2 pt. oysters with liquid
1/4 c. fresh lemon juice	1 10 or 12-oz. package cooked
2 bay leaves, crushed	shelled shrimp
1/4 tsp. pepper	1/4 c. sauterne
1/2 tsp. crushed thyme	1 unpeeled California lemon,
1 tbsp. fresh snipped parsley	thinly sliced

Heat the oil in a large saucepan or Dutch oven and saute the onion and garlic in the oil until tender. Stir in the tomatoes, lemon peel, lemon juice, bay leaves, pepper, thyme, parsley, salt and water and cover. Simmer for 30 minutes. Cut the fish fillets into 2-inch pieces and add to soup. Cut the lobster into 6 or 8 pieces and add to soup. Add the oysters and simmer for 10 minutes. Stir in the shrimp and sauterne and heat just until shrimp are warm. Garnish with sliced lemon and serve immediately. Three frozen lobster-tails, thawed and split, may be substituted for lobster. 6-8 servings.

Bouillabaisse a l'Americaine (above)

TUNA-POTATO CHOWDER

1 can frozen cream of potato soup 2 tbsp. minced onion
1 1/2 c. milk   1 7-oz. can tuna

Combine the soup, milk and onion in a saucepan and heat, stirring, until soup is thawed. Drain and flake the tuna, then stir into the soup mixture. Heat through. 3-4 servings.

Cathy Inmon, Charlotte, North Carolina

CORNED BEEF-PEA SOUP

1 12-oz. can corned beef   1 4-oz. package dried green pea
1 4-oz. can sliced mushrooms   soup
1/4 c. chopped celery   3 c. water
1 tbsp. butter or margarine

Chill and flake the corned beef. Drain the mushrooms, reserving liquid. Cook the mushrooms and celery in butter in a saucepan until celery is tender. Add the soup, water and reserved mushroom liquid and blend. Heat to boiling point, stirring constantly. Add the corned beef and cover. Simmer for 10 minutes. One-half pound fresh mushrooms, sliced, may be substituted for canned mushrooms. 4-6 servings.

Corned Beef-Pea Soup (above)

42

FRANKFURTER STEW

2 med. onions, diced	1/8 tsp. pepper
1 tbsp. shortening	Dash of hot sauce
1 lb. frankfurters	3 potatoes, diced
1 c. cold water	1 tbsp. vinegar
1/8 tsp. salt	

Fry the onions in shortening in a saucepan until brown. Cut each frankfurter into 4 pieces and add to the onions. Add the water, salt, pepper, hot sauce and potatoes and simmer for 30 minutes. Remove from heat and add vinegar. 6-8 servings.

Mrs. W. D. Thompson, Thornton, Texas

RABBIT STEW

1 2-lb. rabbit	1/4 c. chopped onion
1 1/8 c. flour	1 1/2 c. water
1 1/2 tsp. salt	2 stalks celery, chopped
1/8 tsp. pepper	2 sprigs of parsley
1/4 c. shortening	1/2 c. milk

Cut the rabbit into serving pieces. Mix 1 cup flour, salt and pepper and roll rabbit in seasoned flour. Melt the shortening in a frying pan and brown the onion in hot shortening. Remove from frying pan. Brown the rabbit in remaining shortening in the frying pan. Add the water, celery and parsley and cover. Cook over low heat for about 1 hour or until rabbit is almost tender. Add the onion and cook until rabbit is tender. Remove rabbit from frying pan. Mix remaining flour and milk and stir into liquid in frying pan slowly. Cook, stirring, until thickened. Add the rabbit and serve.

Mrs. O. T. Person, Walls, Mississippi

SQUIRREL GUMBO

3 squirrels	1 tbsp. chopped parsley
Oil	1/4 c. chopped celery
1/4 c. flour	1 can tomato paste
1 lge. onion, chopped	1 1/2 c. cut okra
3 cloves of garlic, chopped	Salt and pepper to taste
1 lge. green pepper, chopped	3 qt. water

Cut the squirrels into serving pieces and brown in small amount of oil in a skillet. Remove from skillet. Add flour to remaining oil in the skillet and cook, stirring, until browned. Add remaining ingredients and squirrels and bring to a boil. Reduce heat and cook until squirrels are done. Serve with rice. 6-8 servings.

Mrs. Guy Burton, Jr., Baton Rouge, Louisiana

Stuffed-Rolled Steak with Buttermilk Gravy (page 47)

economy meats

Southern homemakers agree that meat makes the meal. But even these outstanding food managers sometimes feel that it is meat which also breaks the budget. Of course, they want to feed their families nutritious and flavorful meats at least once a day – yet the cost often seems prohibitive.

Perhaps the problem of serving nutritious meat dishes without straining the food dollar is what led to the recipes you'll find in this section – lip-smacking, hearty family dishes that bring you warm compliments, yet cost just pennies a serving. Southerners love their steak – and thrifty homemakers replace expensive cuts of sirloin and porterhouse with more flavorful, less costly cuts. Try Stuffed Flank Steak the next time your family asks for a steak treat – they'll love the unusual flavor . . . and you'll love what it does for your food budget. Marinated Steak is the same kind of dish: low in cost but so high in flavor.

For an unusual flavor combination, serve Baked Pork Chops with Rice. Cooked for long, slow hours, this family favorite in new dress is a wonderful surprise on those cold, rainy nights when everyone wants a hot and filling dish. In fact, this entire section is replete with the kind of recipes you'll be proud to serve your family and guests: creative dishes which use inexpensive meats and a lot of ingenuity to win praise for you!

Country Fare Pot Roast (below)

COUNTRY FARE POT ROAST

1/4 c. flour	1 med. onion, sliced
2 tsp. salt	1 c. water
1 3 to 4-lb. beef arm or blade	1 sm. rutabaga
pot roast	3 stalks celery, cut into 2-inch
3 tbsp. lard or drippings	pieces
6 peppercorns	1 10-oz. package frozen peas

Combine the flour and salt and dredge the roast with seasoned flour. Brown in the lard in a Dutch oven and pour off drippings. Add the peppercorns, onion and water and cover tightly. Cook over low heat for 2 hours. Cut the rutabaga into quarters and cut each quarter into 6 wedge-shaped pieces. Add to roast. Add the celery and cook for 45 minutes longer or until roast is tender and vegetables are done. Cook the peas according to package directions. Remove the roast and vegetables to a heated serving platter. Thicken cooking liquid with additional flour for gravy. Serve peas on platter with the roast and other vegetables. 6 servings.

BARBECUED POT ROAST

1 4-lb. beef pot roast	1 c. sliced onions
2 tbsp. flour	1/4 c. vinegar
1 c. canned tomatoes	1/4 c. lemon juice
1 c. water	1/4 c. hickory-flavored catsup
2 cloves of garlic, minced	2 tbsp. brown sugar
1 tbsp. salt	1 tbsp. Worcestershire sauce
1/2 tsp. pepper	1 tsp. mustard

Dredge the roast with flour and brown well on all sides in small amount of fat in a heavy kettle. Add the tomatoes, water, garlic, salt, pepper and onions and cover. Simmer for 2 hours. Combine remaining ingredients and mix well. Pour over roast and cover. Simmer for about 1 hour and 30 minutes or until the roast is tender.

Doris Sanders, Weir, Mississippi

SPANISH ROAST

1 rump roast	1 can tomato soup
2 cans pimentos	3 soup cans water
3 green peppers	2 bay leaves
3 lge. celery stalks	4 whole cloves
12 sm. whole onions	2 to 3 tsp. salt
8 sm. carrots, sliced	14 sm. potatoes
1 lge. can tomatoes	

Place the roast in a large roasting pan. Bake at 400 degrees until brown and reduce temperature to 350 degrees. Cut the pimentos, green peppers and celery in large pieces and place around roast. Add remaining ingredients except potatoes and cover the roasting pan. Bake until the roast is medium done. Place the potatoes around roast and bake until potatoes are tender and roast is done.

Mrs. G. Harmon English, Hickory, North Carolina

An Oriental Answer to the Problem of Leftovers
Slice leftover roasts into thin strips. Prepare Chinese dishes using these tasty julienne strips.

STUFFED-ROLLED STEAK WITH BUTTERMILK GRAVY

4 c. bread cubes	1/2 c. water
2/3 c. chopped onion	2 beef or vegetable
1/4 c. chopped parsley	bouillon cubes
1/2 c. melted butter	2 tbsp. flour
3 tsp. seasoned salt	1/2 tsp. salt
2 1-lb. slices boned round	2 c. buttermilk
steak, cut 1/4 to 3/8 in. thick	

Combine the bread cubes, onion, parsley, 1/4 cup butter and 1 teaspoon seasoned salt in a bowl and mix. Sprinkle remaining seasoned salt over the steaks and cover each slice of steak with 1/2 of the bread mixture. Roll each up and tie. Place remaining butter in a large frypan over low heat and brown steak rolls on all sides in butter. Add the water and bouillon cubes and cover. Cook over low heat for about 2 hours or until steaks are tender. Remove steaks from frypan. Blend flour and salt into pan drippings. Add the buttermilk and cook, stirring constantly, until thickened. Slice steaks and serve with gravy. 6-8 servings.

Photograph for this recipe on page 44.

STUFFED FLANK STEAK

6 tbsp. shortening
3/4 c. chopped celery
3 tsp. chopped parsley
1/4 c. chopped onion
2 c. bread crumbs

1/2 tsp. savory
1/2 to 3/4 tsp. salt
Pepper to taste
1 boneless flank steak

Melt 4 tablespoons shortening in frypan. Add the celery, parsley and onion and cook until vegetables are tender. Add the crumbs and seasonings and mix well. Spread over steak. Roll as for jelly roll and tie securely with string. Brown on all sides in remaining shortening in a Dutch oven and place a rack under the steak. Cover tightly. Bake at 350 degrees for about 1 hour and 30 minutes. Gravy may be prepared with pan drippings, if desired.

Mrs. Era H. Green, Lexington, Alabama

Dark Brown Gravy
To deepen the color of gravy, stir in a small amount of instant coffee.

GERMAN MEAT ROLL

1   1-lb. boneless chuck steak
Salt and pepper to taste
1 med. onion, thinly sliced

4 slices lean bacon, finely
chopped

Sprinkle both sides of steak with salt and pepper and pound to tenderize. Spread onion and bacon over the steak and roll as for jelly roll. Tie securely with string. Brown in small amount of fat in a skillet. Add small amount of water and cover tightly. Simmer until steak is tender. Place on a warm platter and remove string. Slice and serve with gravy made from pan drippings, if desired.

Mrs. W. E. Smith, Sr., Hardy, Mississippi

BEEF IN NOODLE NESTS

1 egg, beaten
1/2 c. flour
2 lb. beef shoulder, cut in cubes
2 c. oil
2/3 c. brown sugar
1 c. vinegar
1/4 c. molasses
2 med. tomatoes
2 tbsp. cornstarch

1/4 c. pineapple juice
2 green peppers, cut in wide
strips
2 c. drained pineapple chunks
1 tsp. salt
1/8 tsp. pepper
4 cans Chinese noodles
2 egg whites, lightly beaten

Combine the egg, flour and 1 cup water and mix well. Dip the beef cubes into flour mixture and fry in hot oil in a skillet for 8 to 10 minutes. Keep warm. Combine brown sugar, vinegar, molasses and 3/4 cup water in a saucepan and bring to a boil. Reduce heat. Peel the tomatoes, dice and add to vinegar mixture. Simmer for 10 minutes. Blend the cornstarch with pineapple juice and stir into tomato mixture. Cook, stirring constantly, until thickened. Add beef, green peppers, pineapple chunks, salt and pepper and simmer for 15 minutes, stirring occasionally. Toss the noodles with egg whites and shape into nests on a cookie sheet. Bake at 350 degrees for 20 to 30 minutes. Fill with beef mixture and serve. 6 servings.

Mrs. Fred Moon, Pinehurst, Georgia

VEAL CUTLET CORDON BLEU

12 thin slices veal	Flour
Salt and pepper to taste	3 eggs, beaten
6 thin slices Swiss cheese	3/4 c. bread crumbs
6 thin slices boiled ham	3/4 c. butter

Pound the veal slices with a meat hammer until flat, then sprinkle with salt and pepper. Place 1 slice cheese and 1 slice ham on 6 veal slices and cover with remaining veal slices. Pound edges together. Dip in flour, then eggs. Dip in crumbs. Fry in the butter in a skillet until brown on both sides. Place on a platter and garnish with parsley, cherry tomatoes and onion rings. Yield: 6 servings.

Veal Cutlet Cordon Bleu (above)

SPANISH STEAK

1 1/2 lb. round steak	1/4 tsp. pepper
2 tbsp. shortening	2 green peppers
1 can compliment for Swiss Steak	1 tbsp. cornstarch
1 tsp. salt	1 tbsp. water
1/4 tsp. garlic salt	

Cut the steak into 1/4-inch strips and brown in hot shortening in a 10-inch skillet over medium heat. Stir in the compliment, salt, garlic salt and pepper and cover. Simmer for 25 minutes. Cut the green peppers into strips and add to steak mixture. Cook for 20 minutes or until steak is tender. Mix the cornstarch and water until smooth and stir into steak mixture. Cook and stir until thickened. Serve with hot, cooked noodles. 4-6 servings.

Photograph for this recipe on page 2.

BEEF CURRY WITH RICE

4 tbsp. flour	2 1/4 c. water
1 tbsp. curry powder	1 green pepper, chopped
1 tsp. salt	1 onion, chopped
Dash of pepper	2 stalks celery, chopped
2 c. cubed beef	1 c. canned tomatoes
2 tbsp. shortening	3 c. cooked rice

Mix the flour, curry powder, salt and pepper and dredge beef in flour mixture. Reserve remaining flour mixture for gravy. Melt the shortening in a heavy skillet over low heat and brown the beef in shortening, turning frequently. Add 2 cups water and cook for 10 minutes. Add the green pepper, onion, celery and tomatoes. Mix remaining water with reserved flour mixture and stir into beef mixture. Cook until beef is tender and serve over rice.

Mrs. A. L. Dyer, Trenton, Georgia

MARINATED STEAK

1 to 1 1/2 lb. chuck steak	12 sm. white onions, parboiled
Meat tenderizer (opt.)	4 to 6 tomatoes, cut in wedges
2 c. spicy French dressing	4 green peppers, cut in chunks

Cut the steak into 1 1/2-inch cubes, sprinkle with tenderizer and place in a bowl. Pour 1 cup French dressing over the steak and refrigerate for at least 2 hours. Place the onions, tomatoes and green peppers in a bowl and add remaining French dressing. Refrigerate for 2 hours. Drain the steak and vegetables. Place the steak cubes, onions, tomato wedges and green pepper chunks alternately on skewers. Broil to desired doneness. May be grilled over charcoal, if desired. 4-6 servings.

Mrs. Martha Brown, Gallatin, Tennessee

VEGETABLES AND BEEF

2 lb. boneless stew beef	12 sm. white onions
1/2 c. flour	12 sm. potatoes
3 tsp. salt	4 med. carrots
4 tbsp. shortening	1 med. green pepper
2 1/2 c. water	1/2 tsp. pepper
1 bay leaf	

Trim excess fat from the beef and discard. Combine the flour and salt in a paper bag. Add the beef and shake to coat well. Brown in the shortening in a Dutch oven or a 3-quart saucepan. Add the water and bay leaf and cover. Cook over moderate heat for 1 hour and 30 minutes or until beef is almost tender. Peel the onions and potatoes. Cut the carrots into 1 1/2-inch lengths and green pepper into 3/4-inch strips. Add the onions, potatoes, carrots and green pepper to beef and cover. Cook for 30 minutes or until vegetables are tender. Add the pepper and serve hot. 6 servings.

MOCK FILET MIGNON

1 1/2 lb. lean ground beef	1 1/2 tsp. salt
2 c. cooked rice	1/4 tsp. pepper
1 c. minced onions	8 slices bacon
1 clove of garlic, crushed	1 can cream of mushroom soup
2 tbsp. Worcestershire sauce	1/4 c. milk

Combine all ingredients except the bacon, soup and milk and mix well. Divide into 8 equal parts and shape into round patties about 3/4 inch thick. Wrap bacon around edge and secure with toothpicks. Place on an ungreased cookie pan. Bake at 450 degrees for 15 minutes or until done. Mix the soup and milk in a saucepan and heat through, stirring constantly. 8 servings.

Mock Filet Mignon (above)

CARROTBURGERS

2 c. grated carrots	1 lb. ground beef
1/4 c. grated onion	1 1/2 tsp. salt
1/4 c. grated green pepper	1/4 tsp. pepper

Combine all ingredients and shape into patties. Place in a shallow baking pan. Broil 3 inches from heat for 8 minutes. Turn and broil for 5 minutes longer. 8 servings.

Mrs. Walter Cox, Malvern, Arkansas

Retaining Food Moisture During Cooking
To prevent food from drying out or burning in a saucepan, simply place a layer of waxed paper between saucepan and lid. This old Japanese cooking technique, known as **otoshi-buta**, will restrict excessive loss of liquid and shorten cooking time.

MEAT LOAF WITH SPICY SAUCE

1 1/2 lb. ground beef	1 tbsp. Worcestershire sauce
1 c. corn flakes	1/4 tsp. salt
2 egg yolks	1/2 c. water
1/4 tsp. instant minced onion	1 tbsp. mustard
1/4 tsp. celery seed	2 tbsp. vinegar
1 c. tomato paste	2 tbsp. brown sugar
1/2 c. milk	Dash of pepper

Combine the beef, corn flakes, egg yolks, onion, celery seed, 1/2 cup tomato paste, milk, Worcestershire sauce and salt and mix well. Shape in a loaf and place in a baking pan. Combine the water, remaining tomato paste, mustard, vinegar, brown sugar and pepper and mix well. Pour over the loaf. Bake at 350 degrees for 1 hour and 30 minutes.

Mrs. John Carroll, La Follette, Tennessee

TAMALE PIE

1/2 c. chopped onions	1 tbsp. sugar
1/2 c. chopped green pepper	2 tsp. chili powder
3/4 lb. ground beef	Dash of pepper
1 12-oz. can whole kernel corn	1 1/2 tsp. salt
2 8-oz. cans seasoned tomato sauce	1 1/2 c. shredded process cheese
1/2 c. chopped, pitted ripe olives	3/4 c. yellow cornmeal
1 clove of garlic, minced	2 c. cold water
	1 tbsp. butter

Cook the onions and green pepper in small amount of hot fat in a skillet till just tender. Add the ground beef and brown lightly. Spoon off excess fat. Drain the corn and stir into beef mixture. Add the tomato sauce, olives, garlic, sugar, chili powder, pepper and 1 teaspoon salt and simmer for 20 to 25 minutes or till thickened. Add the cheese and stir till melted. Pour into 10 x 6 x 1 1/2-inch baking dish. Bake, covered, at 375 degrees for 1 hour and 15 minutes. Stir the cornmeal and remaining salt into cold water in a saucepan. Cook, stirring, till thickened. Add butter and mix well. Spoon over the beef mixture in narrow strips and bake for 35 to 40 minutes longer.

Mrs. Eva C. Norton, Jacksonville, Florida

UPSIDE-DOWN HAM-YAM LOAF

5 med. Louisiana yams	1 med. onion, finely chopped
3/4 c. (firmly packed) light	2 tbsp. finely chopped
brown sugar	green pepper
3 med. tart cooking apples	2 tbsp. parsley
2 tbsp. butter	1/2 tsp. sage
Nutmeg to taste	1/2 tsp. salt
1 lb. ground cooked ham	1/4 tsp. pepper
1 lb. ground beef round	1 egg, slightly beaten
1 lb. ground veal shoulder	3/4 c. apple juice
1 c. soft bread crumbs	

Cook the yams, covered, in boiling, salted water for 15 to 20 minutes, then drain. Peel and slice 1/2 inch thick. Sprinkle the brown sugar over bottom of a lightly greased 9 x 13-inch pan. Peel and core the apples, then slice 1/2 inch thick. Place the yam slices on brown sugar and place apple slices on yam slices. Dot with butter and sprinkle with nutmeg. Mix the ground meats, bread crumbs, onion, green pepper, parsley, seasonings, egg and apple juice and press on top of apples. Bake in 350-degree oven for 1 hour. Pour off drippings carefully and reserve. Place a platter on top of baking dish and invert so loaf rests, yam side up, on platter. Lift off baking dish. Spoon some of the reserved drippings over top. Serve remaining drippings as gravy with ham loaf. 6-8 servings.

Upside-Down Ham-Yam Loaf (above)

BAKED PORK CHOPS AND RICE

6 pork chops	1 tsp. pepper
1 c. rice	1 lge. onion, chopped fine
3 c. hot water	1 can cream of mushroom soup
1 tsp. salt	1 lge. green pepper, thinly sliced

Trim fat from the pork chops and brown the chops on both sides in a skillet. Mix the rice, water, salt, pepper, onion, undiluted soup and green pepper in a shallow 2-quart baking dish. Place pork chops on top and cover with foil. Bake in 375-degree oven for 45 minutes to 1 hour or until chops and rice are tender.

Mrs. Richard Steeves, Blytheville, Arkansas

CRANBERRY PORK CHOPS

2 pork chops, 1 in. thick	1/2 tsp. lemon juice
1 tbsp. cooking oil	Salt and pepper to taste
1 tbsp. flour	1 c. fresh cranberries, halved
1/4 c. red wine	1/2 c. honey
1/4 c. water	Grated rind of 1 sm. lemon

Brown the pork chops on each side in hot oil in a skillet and sprinkle with flour. Pour the wine, water and lemon juice over chops and season with salt and pepper. Place the chops in a single layer in a greased casserole. Stir the liquid in skillet to loosen all brown bits, then pour over and around the chops. Mix the cranberry halves, honey and lemon rind and place over chops. Cover. Bake at 350 degrees for 1 hour. Place the pork chops on a platter and spoon the sauce over chops. Recipe may be doubled or tripled.

Photograph for this recipe on page 151.

BAKED HAM WITH APPLESAUCE GLAZE

1 4-lb. picnic ham	1 tsp. bottled mustard
1 can applesauce	1/8 tsp. cinnamon
1/2 c. orange marmalade	

Place the ham, fat side up, in a shallow baking pan. Bake in 350-degree oven for 1 hour and 30 minutes. Mix remaining ingredients and spread half the mixture on ham. Bake for 30 minutes. Spread with remaining applesauce mixture and bake for 30 minutes longer. Garnish with spiced crab apples.

Mrs. Scott Bunker, Mt. Airy, North Carolina

HUNGARIAN-STUFFED CABBAGE

2 lb. ground pork	1 1/3 c. rice
1 4-in. square slab bacon, ground	Tomato juice
1 lge. onion, chopped	1 med. cabbage
2 eggs, beaten	1 pt. sauerkraut
1 tsp. pepper	

Mix first 6 ingredients with 1/3 cup tomato juice. Remove core from the cabbage and place cabbage in a saucepan. Cover with boiling water and cook for about 10 minutes. Remove about 3/4 of the leaves and cut out heavy vein at the base. Fill leaves with pork mixture, roll up and secure with picks. Chop remaining cabbage and mix with the sauerkraut. Place half the cabbage and sauerkraut in a large saucepan. Place cabbage rolls on top and cover with remaining cabbage and sauerkraut. Add enough water to cover and bring to a boil. Cook over medium heat for 1 hour. Add enough tomato juice to cover and simmer for 45 minutes longer.

Mrs. Robert Snyder, Houston, Texas

STUFFED PORK ROAST

1 pkg. herb-seasoned stuffing mix	1 3 1/2 to 4-lb. boneless pork loin

Prepare the stuffing mix according to package directions. Cut the loin lengthwise to within 1 inch of other side. Place the stuffing in the center of the loin lengthwise. Fold loin over and tie securely with string. Place in a roasting pan and add 2 cups water. Cover. Bake at 325 degrees for 2 hours. Uncover and bake until brown, basting occasionally.

Stuffed Pork Roast (above)

ORANGE-GLAZED PORK ROAST

1/2 6-oz. can concentrated   2 tbsp. steak sauce
    orange juice   1 4 to 5-lb. loin pork roast
2 tbsp. melted margarine

Blend the orange juice with margarine and steak sauce. Place the pork roast in a baking pan and brush with orange mixture. Bake in 350-degree oven for about 2 hours and 30 minutes, brushing with orange mixture every 30 minutes.

Mrs. Frank L. Love, Miami, Florida

ROAST PORK

1 2-lb. pork neck or loin   1 tsp. caraway seed
Salt to taste

Score the pork and place in a baking pan. Season with salt and sprinkle with caraway seed. Add small amount of water to baking pan. Bake at 350 degrees for about 1 hour and 10 minutes or until done, basting occasionally with pan drippings.

Mrs. Eleanor Quinn, Memphis, Tennessee

MEAL-IN-A-DISH

1 lb. sliced ham   Salt and pepper to taste
2 lge. potatoes, sliced thin   1 c. milk
1 lge. onion, sliced thin   Grated Parmesan or Cheddar cheese
2 tbsp. margarine

Brown the ham on both sides in a skillet and place in a casserole. Cover with alternate layers of potatoes and onion. Dot with margarine and season with salt and pepper. Add the milk. Bake at 350 degrees for 45 minutes or until potatoes are tender. Cover with cheese and bake until brown.

Lillian V. Byrd, San Antonio, Texas

SCRAPPLE

1 lb. bulk sausage, crumbled   2 tsp. salt
3 c. water   1/8 tsp. pepper
1 c. cornmeal

Brown the sausage in a saucepan and pour off fat. Add 2 cups water and heat to boiling point. Combine the cornmeal, salt and pepper with remaining water and add to boiling sausage mixture, stirring constantly. Reduce heat and simmer for 10 minutes, stirring frequently. Pour into a greased loaf pan and chill until firm. Cut in 1/2-inch slices and fry in small amount of fat until brown. Serve with jelly.

Mrs. J. W. Williams, Concord, Tennessee

SQUASH AND SAUSAGE

1 lb. bulk pork sausage	1/2 c. milk
1 sm. clove of garlic, crushed	1 tbsp. snipped parsley
4 c. sliced summer squash	1/2 tsp. crushed oregano
1/2 c. dry bread crumbs	1/2 tsp. salt
1/2 c. grated Parmesan cheese	2 beaten eggs

Cook the sausage and garlic in a skillet until brown and drain off excess fat. Cook the squash in small amount of water until tender and drain. Stir into the sausage mixture. Add the bread crumbs, cheese, milk, parsley, oregano and salt and mix well. Fold in the eggs and place in a shallow baking dish. Bake at 350 degrees for about 30 minutes. 4-6 servings.

Mrs. S. M. Kolbohn, Fort Worth, Texas

SAUSAGE SUPPER SQUARES

1 1/2 lb. link pork sausage	1 12-oz. can whole kernel
1 3/4 c. sifted all-purpose	corn
flour	Milk
4 tsp. baking powder	1/2 c. whole bran cereal
1 tsp. salt	3 eggs
1 1/2 tbsp. sugar	

Cook the sausage in a frypan over low heat until browned and thoroughly cooked. Drain and reserve 1/4 cup drippings. Sift the flour, baking powder, salt and sugar together. Drain the corn and reserve liquid. Add enough milk to reserved liquid to make 1 1/2 cups liquid and pour in a mixing bowl. Add reserved drippings, whole bran cereal, corn and eggs and beat well. Add sifted ingredients and beat until smooth. Pour into a greased 15 1/2 x 10 1/2 x 1-inch baking pan and place the sausage links on batter, arranging in a uniform pattern. Bake in a 450-degree oven for about 20 minutes or until golden brown. Cut into squares and serve hot with syrup or hot seasoned cream sauce.

Sausage Supper Squares (above)

LAMB SHANKS WITH MUSHROOM SAUCE

4 lamb shanks	1 tsp. celery seed
2 tbsp. salad oil	1 tsp. salt
2 onions, sliced	1/8 tsp. pepper
1 pkg. mushroom soup mix	1/2 tsp. dry mustard
2 c. water	

Cook the lamb shanks in hot oil in a skillet over low heat until browned. Add the onions and cook for 5 minutes. Drain off drippings. Combine the remaining ingredients and stir into the lamb mixture. Cover skillet. Cook over low heat for 50 to 60 minutes or until the lamb is tender.

Mrs. S. M. Kirson, Key West Florida

ORANGE-GLAZED LAMB CHOPS

4 shoulder lamb chops, cut 3/4 in. thick	2 tbsp. brown sugar
Salt and pepper to taste	2 tbsp. frozen orange juice concentrate

Preheat oven to 500 degrees. Place the lamb chops on rack of a broiler pan and place broiler pan 3 inches from heat. Broil for 6 to 8 minutes or until the lamb chops are browned. Turn the lamb chops and broil for about 3 minutes. Season with the salt and pepper. Combine the brown sugar and orange juice and spread on chops. Broil for about 2 minutes longer or until chops are done. 4 servings.

Susie Nelson, Clinton, Tennessee

Sour Cream Substitute for the Pocket and Pound Conscious
Combine 1/4 cup water and 1 cup cottage cheese in an electric blender for 20 seconds at high speed, or until cottage cheese is liquefied. Add 1 teaspoon lemon juice, 1/2 teaspoon salt, and chives or onion or garlic salt to taste.

BRAIN LOAF

2 lb. beef or pork brains	7 eggs
1 env. unflavored gelatin	1 1/4 c. bread crumbs
2 tbsp. cold water	1 c. heavy cream
2 tbsp. butter	5 hard-boiled eggs, chopped

Cook the brains in boiling, salted water in a saucepan for about 20 minutes or until done. Drain and cut into small pieces. Soften gelatin in cold water in a cup. Melt the butter in a large skillet. Mix 4 eggs and 3 egg yolks and beat slightly. Add the brains and bread crumbs and stir well. Add the cream, hard-boiled eggs and gelatin and pour into skillet. Cook over low heat, stirring constantly, until eggs are set. Beat the egg whites until stiff and fold into the brains mixture. Place in a casserole and cover. Bake at 350 degrees for 30 minutes.

Mrs. Meredith J. Cox, Richmond, Kentucky

SOUTHERN FRANKFURTER DINNER

1 med. onion, cut into rings	2 c. canned tomatoes
1/3 c. diced green pepper	Dash of salt and pepper
1 tbsp. shortening	1 8 1/2-oz. package corn
1/2 lb. frankfurters,	muffin mix
thinly sliced	

Fry the onion rings and green pepper in shortening in a frypan until tender, then add the frankfurters, tomatoes, salt and pepper. Pour into an 8-inch square baking dish. Prepare corn muffin mix according to package directions and spoon over frankfurter mixture. Bake at 400 degrees for 20 to 25 minutes or till golden brown.

Mrs. Bob Wester, Darlington, South Carolina

SKILLET MEAL

1 c. chicken broth	1/4 tsp. cinnamon
3 slices frozen fish, thawed	1 tsp. salt
1/4 c. oil	1/4 tsp. pepper
1/2 lb. ham or Canadian bacon	1 lb. cooked chicken, cut
1/4 lb. pork sausage or	in long strips
knackworst sliced	1 10-oz. package frozen
2 cloves of garlic, sliced	lima beans
1 c. chopped tomatoes,	1 6-oz. jar marinated
drained	artichoke halves
1 pinch of saffron	3 hard-cooked eggs, sliced

Pour the broth into a skillet and heat to boiling point. Add the fish and poach for 3 to 4 minutes or until done. Remove from skillet. Reserve broth. Wipe out skillet and add oil. Fry the ham and sausage slices until brown, then remove from skillet. Saute the garlic and tomatoes in the same oil. Add seasonings, chicken, reserved broth, sausage, ham, lima beans, artichokes and fish and cook until thick. Garnish with eggs. 6-8 servings.

Skillet Meal (above)

Bern Plate (below)

BERN PLATE

1/2 lb. slab bacon	I carrot, quartered
2 16 or 17-oz. cans sauerkraut	I leek
1 1 1/2 to 2-lb. sliced	1 c. water
smoked pork butt	1/2 tsp. salt
1/2 lb. bottom round of beef	1 pr. Italian sausages
2 stalks celery, quartered	1 4-oz. can Vienna sausages

Cut the bacon in thick slices. Combine the sauerkraut, bacon and smoked pork in a saucepan and bring to a boil. Reduce heat and cover. Simmer for 1 hour and 30 minutes. Cut the beef into 1/2-inch slices. Combine the beef, celery, carrot, leek, water and salt in a saucepan and cover. Bring to a boil and simmer for about 1 hour or until beef is tender. Combine the Italian sausages and Vienna sausages and liquid in a small saucepan and cover. Cook over low heat for about 20 minutes or until thoroughly done, adding several tablespoons water, if necessary. Drain the beef and discard vegetables. Slice the sausages. Arrange the sauerkraut in center of large serving platter and arrange meat slices alternately around edge. 6-8 servings.

SWEET-SOUR HEARTS

2 veal hearts	6 tbsp. vinegar
2 tbsp. flour	3 tbsp. sugar
2 tbsp. shortening	1/4 tsp. pepper
1 sm. onion, chopped	3 c. water
1 tsp. salt	

Clean the hearts, removing membrane and large veins, and cut into 1/2-inch cubes. Brown the flour in shortening in a skillet. Add hearts and remaining ingredients and cover. Simmer for 1 hour and 30 minutes or until the hearts are tender. Serve with noodles or rice. 4 servings.

Mrs. Clayton Ernst, Great Lakes Naval Training Center, Illinois

SPICED BEEF TONGUE

1 lge. beef tongue	1 tbsp. cloves
1 tsp. salt	1 tbsp. allspice
1 peppercorn	1/2 c. vinegar
2 tbsp. sugar	

Place the tongue in a large saucepan and cover with boiling water. Add the salt and peppercorn, then cook until tender. Remove the tongue from the water, pull off and discard skin. Place tongue in a separate saucepan and add the sugar, spices, vinegar and 1 cup water. Simmer, turning frequently, until liquid has evaporated. Chill the tongue and slice thinly. Garnish with lemon and parsley. 8-10 servings.

Carrie Dee Drew, West Monroe, Louisiana

LIVER IN CASSEROLE

2 carrots, cut in cubes	Salt to taste
2 potatoes, cut in cubes	Flour
1 onion, chopped	4 tbsp. butter
1 can English peas, drained	2 c. milk
1 lb. sliced beef liver	

Place the carrots, potatoes and onion in a saucepan and cover with water. Bring to a boil and simmer for about 8 minutes or until partially done. Drain and add peas. Season the liver with salt and dredge with flour. Brown in the butter in a skillet and remove from skillet. Cut liver into cubes. Add 2 tablespoons flour to drippings in the skillet and stir well. Add the milk slowly and cook, stirring constantly, until thickened. Place alternate layers of carrot mixture and liver in a casserole and pour gravy over top. Bake at 325 degrees for 1 hour. 6 servings.

Jewell Harrison, Grand Prairie, Texas

Easy-to-Store Liver Slices
After removing liver from market wrappings, make a stack of the individual slices, separating each with 2 sheets of waxed paper, and bacon, if desired. Wrap stack in foil; freeze. Dislodge the number of slices needed for a meal, season, then broil in a moderate oven (350 degrees) for 20 minutes, or until tender.

SPICED LUNCHEON MEAT

1 can luncheon meat	1/2 tsp. nutmeg (opt.)
1 med. can crushed pineapple	1/3 c. honey or maple syrup
1/2 tsp. cinnamon	1 tbsp. cornstarch
1/2 tsp. cloves	

Slice the luncheon meat and place in a baking pan. Drain the pineapple and reserve juice. Place reserved juice in a saucepan and add the spices and honey. Bring to a boil. Mix cornstarch with small amount of water and stir into the honey mixture. Add the pineapple and spread over meat. Bake at 350 degrees for about 20 minutes.

Kay McAlhany, Grovetown, Georgia

Best Barbecued Turkey (page 80)

low-cost poultry

Of all the bargains in today's grocery stores, poultry is one of the biggest. Only a generation ago, chicken and other poultry were special treats, reserved throughout the Southland for "company's coming" Sunday dinners. Today poultry constitutes one of the biggest budget-savers in the supermarket.

The southern touch with poultry has always been near-legendary and the recipe collection you'll find in the following section convincingly proves the truth of this legend.

Chicken, of course, comes in for plenty of attention. Serve it to your family as Arkansas Chicken and Rice, two traditional favorite southern foods combined into one flavorful casserole. Or prepare Skillet Barbecued Chicken, a quick-and-easy timesaver as well as a great budget-trimmer. No section on southern-style chicken is complete without recipes for fried chicken — and old-time Herbed Fried Chicken is just one of the many low-cost fried chicken recipes awaiting you.

Turkey is featured in a variety of recipes, too, from Festive Turkey and Dressing to Turkey Croquettes and Turkey-stuffed Green Peppers, an unusual blend of wild and piquant flavors. Whatever the recipe you choose to prepare, you can be certain that it's one of the very finest recipes from the homes of America's finest cooks — southern homemakers!

Chicken Basque (below)

CHICKEN BASQUE

2 lge. chicken breasts, split	1/2 c. chopped green pepper
Flour	1/2 c. chopped onion
1/3 c. diet imitation margarine	1 3-oz. can sliced mushrooms, drained
1 c. chicken bouillon	1 tsp. oregano leaves
1 8-oz. can tomato sauce	1 tsp. salt
	1/8 tsp. pepper

Dust the chicken pieces lightly with flour. Melt the diet margarine in a large skillet over low heat. Add the chicken and brown. Add remaining ingredients and cover. Cook over low heat for 20 minutes. Remove cover and cook for about 10 minutes longer or until chicken is done. 4 servings.

ARKANSAS CHICKEN AND RICE

2 lge. fryers, disjointed	1 sm. onion, minced
1/4 c. olive oil	1 clove of garlic, minced
1/4 c. butter	1 No. 2 can tomatoes
2 c. rice	

Cook the chickens in boiling water until tender. Drain and reserve stock. Heat the oil and butter in a skillet. Brown the chicken in oil mixture and drain on paper towels. Brown the rice, onion and garlic in same skillet and add tomatoes. Place rice mixture in a deep casserole and cover with chicken. Skim the fat from the chicken stock and pour enough stock into the casserole to cover rice mixture. Cover the casserole. Bake in a 350-degree oven for about 1 hour, adding stock, if needed. Garnish with parsley and pimento strips. 7-8 servings.

Mrs. Van H. Stevens, Searcy, Arkansas

CHICKEN AND DRESSING

1 hen	3 onions, diced
1 loaf bread, crumbled	2 tsp. sage
1 recipe baked corn bread, crumbled	Salt and pepper to taste
	1 tbsp. melted butter

Cook the chicken in boiling water until tender but still firm. Drain and reserve 2 quarts broth. Combine remaining ingredients with reserved broth and mix well. Place some of the dressing in cavity of chicken and place chicken in a baking pan. Place remaining dressing around chicken. Bake at 350 degrees until dressing is done and chicken is brown.

Evelyn Cunningham, Searcy, Arkansas

CHICKEN CROQUETTES DELUXE

1/2 c. mayonnaise	1 tbsp. minced parsley
1/2 tsp. salt	2 tbsp. water
1 tbsp. minced onion	2 c. chopped cooked chicken
1/8 tsp. pepper	1 c. soft bread crumbs
1 tsp. Worcestershire sauce	Sifted dried bread crumbs

Combine the mayonnaise, salt, onion, pepper, Worcestershire sauce and parsley in a bowl and stir in water. Add the chicken and soft bread crumbs and mix well. Let stand for 5 minutes. Shape into 6 croquettes and roll in dried bread crumbs. Place on baking sheet lined with heavy brown paper. Bake at 450 degrees for about 20 minutes or until browned. One cup cooked rice may be substituted for soft bread crumbs.

Mrs. Ernest Jackson, Bessemer, Alabama

CHICKEN STRATA

10 slices bread	Salt and pepper to taste
2 c. diced cooked chicken	4 eggs, beaten
1/2 c. mayonnaise	3 c. milk
1 c. chopped celery	1 can mushroom soup
1 green pepper, chopped	Grated Cheddar cheese
1 med. onion, chopped	Paprika to taste

Dice 4 slices bread and place in a greased 13 x 9 x 2-inch baking dish. Combine the chicken, mayonnaise, celery, green pepper, onion, salt and pepper and place over diced bread. Cut crust from remaining bread and place bread over chicken. Mix the eggs with milk and pour over bread. Refrigerate overnight. Bake at 350 degrees for 15 minutes. Pour the mushroom soup over top and cover with cheese. Sprinkle with paprika and bake for 1 hour longer.

Mrs. Jack Brown, Birmingham, Alabama

YELLOW RICE AND CHICKEN

1 3 to 3 1/2-lb. chicken	1 bay leaf
1/2 c. olive oil	2 tbsp. salt
1 med. onion, diced	2 c. rice
2 cloves of garlic, pressed	1/2 tsp. saffron
3/4 c. tomatoes	1 green pepper, diced
1 1/2 qt. chicken broth or	1 sm. can tiny peas
water	2 pimentos, cut in strips

Cut the chicken in serving pieces and brown in the oil in a skillet. Remove from skillet. Cook the onion and garlic in oil remaining in the skillet until tender. Add the chicken, tomatoes and broth and cook for 5 minutes. Add the bay leaf, salt, rice, saffron and green pepper and mix. Place in a baking dish. Bake in 375-degree oven for 30 minutes or until rice is tender and garnish with the peas and pimentos. Three or 4 drops of yellow food coloring may be substituted for the saffron. 6 servings.

Mrs. Louise W. Henson, Bessemer, Alabama

OAHU PEACHES AND CHICKEN

1/2 c. soy sauce	1 3 to 3 1/2-lb. frying chicken,
1 tbsp. vinegar	disjointed
1/2 tsp. instant minced onion	1/3 c. cornstarch
1/2 tsp. powdered ginger	1/3 c. flour
1/2 tsp. seasoned salt	1/2 c. shortening
Dash of garlic powder	1 1-lb. 13-oz. can cling peach halves

Combine the soy sauce, vinegar, onion, ginger, salt and garlic powder and pour over the chicken in a shallow glass dish or pan. Let stand for several hours at room temperature or refrigerate overnight, spooning marinade over chicken occasionally. Combine the cornstarch and flour. Remove chicken from marinade

Oahu Peaches and Chicken (above)

and roll in the cornstarch mixture. Brown on all sides in hot shortening in a skillet, then arrange in a shallow pan or casserole. Bake in 350-degree oven for 55 minutes. Drain the peaches and spoon marinade into centers of peach halves. Place peaches in pan with chicken and bake for 5 minutes longer. 4-5 servings.

CHICKEN SOPA

1 6-lb. hen	1 can green chili peppers,
1 can chicken bouillon or	chopped
consomme	1 pkg. tostados
2 cans cream of mushroom soup	1 lb. sharp cheese, grated
1 onion, diced	

Cook the chicken in boiling water until tender, then drain and cool. Remove chicken from bones and cut in small pieces. Add the bouillon, soup, onion and chili peppers and mix well. Place alternate layers of chicken mixture and tostados in a greased 2-quart casserole and top with cheese. Bake at 375 degrees for 30 minutes. 12 servings.

Mrs. M. Stockstill, Santo, Texas

No Wasted Chicken Parts
Cut a whole chicken into parts, frying only the pieces that will be eaten, and stewing the wings, liver, and neck pieces that remain. These parts may be used for dressing, dumplings, or salad; the broth, for soup.

PECAN CHICKEN

1 c. prepared biscuit mix	1 2 1/2 to 3-lb. fryer
2 tsp. paprika	1/2 c. evaporated milk
1/2 tsp. poultry seasoning	1 c. melted butter
1/2 c. finely chopped pecans	

Combine the biscuit mix, seasonings and pecans in a bowl. Cut the chicken in serving pieces and dip in evaporated milk. Coat with pecan mixture. Place in 13 x 9 x 2-inch baking pan and pour butter over chicken. Bake at 350 degrees for 1 hour.

Mrs. M. H. Savage, Dallas, Texas

SOUTHERN-STYLE SMOTHERED CHICKEN

1 3-lb. fryer	2 to 3 tbsp. flour
Salt and pepper to taste	2 c. boiling water
Butter or margarine	

Split the chicken down the back and season with salt and pepper. Place in a baking pan, skin side up, and dot with butter. Sprinkle flour over the chicken and pour water into pan. Bake at 450 degrees for 15 minutes, then cover. Reduce temperature to 350 degrees and bake for 1 hour longer. Juices may be thickened for gravy, if desired.

Mrs. B. N. Truduck, Ridge Spring, South Carolina

CHICKEN PIZZAS

1 clove of garlic, minced	1 tsp. crushed oregano
2/3 c. Spanish-style tomato sauce	1 10-count pkg. refrigerator biscuits
1 1/2 c. diced cooked chicken	2 tbsp. grated Parmesan cheese
2 tbsp. diced onion	

Mix the garlic and tomato sauce and let stand for 1 hour. Add the chicken, onion and oregano and mix well. Cut the biscuits in half and place on lightly greased baking sheet. Flatten into 2 1/2-inch circles and form a rim around each circle. Spread chicken mixture on biscuits and sprinkle with Parmesan cheese. Bake at 425 degrees for 10 minutes or until lightly browned.

Mrs. Delbert Thompson, Tyler, Texas

SPANISH CHICKEN

1/2 c. flour	1/4 c. chopped onion
2 tsp. salt	1/4 c. chopped green pepper
1 fryer, disjointed	2 c. milk
1/4 c. shortening	1/4 tsp. pepper
1/2 c. rice	1/8 tsp. chili powder

Mix the flour and 1 teaspoon salt and dredge chicken with flour mixture. Brown in shortening in a skillet and remove from skillet. Brown the rice, onion and green pepper in same skillet, then place in a baking pan. Place chicken on rice mixture. Mix the milk, remaining salt, pepper and chili powder and pour over chicken. Cover. Bake at 350 degrees for 1 hour and 15 minutes or until rice is done.

Mrs. Lee Tschirhart, Castroville, Texas

BRAISED CHICKEN AND FRESH VEGETABLES

1 3 to 4-lb. chicken	1 c. fresh snap beans
2 tbsp. shortening	1 c. fresh green peas
2 c. boiling water	1/2 tsp. pepper
3 tsp. salt	2 tbsp. flour
12 sm. whole white onions	3 tbsp. cold water
4 stalks celery	1/4 c. pimento strips
1/2 med. green pepper	

Cut the chicken into serving pieces and brown on all sides in hot shortening in a Dutch oven or saucepan. Add the boiling water and salt and cover. Cook for 10 minutes. Peel the onions. Cut the celery into 1-inch pieces and green pepper into 1/2-inch strips. Add the onions, celery and green pepper to the chicken and cover. Cook for 25 minutes. Cut the beans into 1-inch pieces and add to chicken mixture. Add the peas and pepper and cook for 15 minutes. Blend flour with cold water to a smooth paste. Stir into the chicken mixture and cook for 1 to 2 minutes longer. Add pimento and serve hot.

LEMON-BARBECUED CHICKEN

2 2-lb. broilers	
1/2 c. melted butter	1/2 med. onion, chopped
2/3 c. lemon juice	1 tsp. salt
2 cloves of garlic, minced	1/2 tsp. cracked pepper

Cut the chicken into halves or quarters and place on grill over hot coals. Combine remaining ingredients in a saucepan and heat through. Cook chicken for about 40 minutes or until tender, turning and brushing with sauce every 5 minutes. 4-6 servings.

Mrs. Wilmer E. Harper, Lucedale, Mississippi

HAWAIIAN-BARBECUED CHICKEN

2 c. canned applesauce	1/2 tsp. dry mustard
1/2 c. apple juice	1/2 c. toasted slivered almonds
2 tbsp. lemon juice	1 broiler-fryer, cut in quarters
1 tsp. grated lemon rind	1/4 c. melted butter or margarine
1/2 c. (packed) brown sugar	1/2 tsp. salt

Combine the applesauce, apple juice, lemon juice, lemon rind, brown sugar, mustard and almonds. Brush the chicken with butter and season with salt. Brown chicken on both sides on grill about 4 inches from heat. Tear a 2-foot length of 18-inch wide heavy-duty aluminum foil and fold in half lengthwise. Turn edges up 2 inches all around and fold corners closed. Place the chicken in the foil pan and place on grill. Pour applesauce mixture over chicken and cover pan loosely with foil. Cook for 45 minutes, turning chicken once and spooning sauce over chicken. Remove foil cover and cook for 15 minutes. Spoon sauce left in pan over chicken and serve. 4 servings.

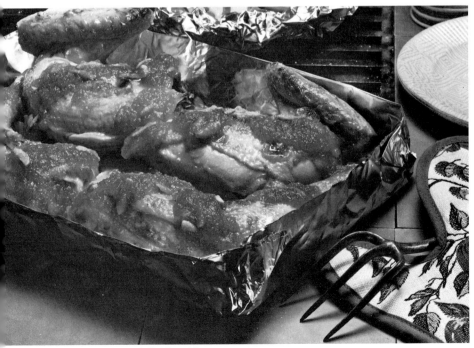

Hawaiian-Barbecued Chicken (above)

SKILLET-BARBECUED CHICKEN

1/4 c. salad oil	1/2 tsp. pepper
2 tbsp. brown sugar	1/2 tsp. celery seed
2 tbsp. vinegar	1/2 tsp. parsley flakes
1 tsp. Worcestershire sauce	1/4 c. water
1/4 tsp. garlic salt	12 pieces of chicken
1 tsp. salt	

Combine all ingredients except chicken in a frypan. Add the chicken and simmer for about 45 minutes or until chicken is tender, adding water, if needed. Remove chicken to a platter. Drain oil from frypan. Add small amount of hot water to frypan and stir to loosen brown particles. Pour over chicken.

Mrs. Andrew Mayer, Hattiesburg, Mississippi

SAVORY BARBECUED CHICKEN

1/2 c. catsup	4 tbsp. brown sugar
3 tbsp. margarine	1 tsp. mustard
1 tbsp. lemon juice	1 tbsp. paprika
2 tbsp. Worcestershire sauce	2 tsp. pepper
1 tbsp. chili powder	1 tsp. salt or to taste
4 tbsp. vinegar	1 3 1/2-lb. chicken,
5 tbsp. water	disjointed

Combine all ingredients except chicken. Dip chicken in sauce and place in baking pan lined with aluminum foil. Cover with foil. Bake at 350 degrees for 1 hour and 30 minutes, basting frequently with remaining sauce.

Mrs. Don L. Glisson, Corinth, Mississippi

TANGY BARBECUED CHICKEN

1/2 c. melted butter	3 tsp. barbecue flavoring
1/2 c. lemon juice	3 tbsp. barbecue sauce
3/4 c. wine vinegar	1 tbsp. salt
1/4 c. soy sauce	1 3-lb. chicken, quartered
1 tsp. meat tenderizer	

Mix the butter, lemon juice, vinegar, soy sauce, meat tenderizer, barbecue flavoring, barbecue sauce and salt. Add the chicken and marinate for 3 hours. Cook on barbecue grill for 45 minutes or until tender, basting with sauce frequently. 4 servings.

Mrs. Mark Savage, Bisbee, Arizona

WEST'S POINT CHICKEN

1 fryer, disjointed	3 tbsp. catsup
Salt and pepper to taste	2 tbsp. Worcestershire sauce

3 tbsp. brown sugar
4 tbsp. water
4 tbsp. lemon juice

1 tsp. mustard
1 tsp. chili powder
1/4 tsp. garlic salt

Season the chicken with salt and pepper. Combine remaining ingredients in a saucepan and simmer for about 5 minutes. Dip chicken in sauce and place in an aluminum foil-lined 9 x 13-inch baking pan. Pour remaining sauce over chicken and cover the pan with foil. Bake at 450 degrees for 15 minutes. Reduce temperature to 350 degrees and bake for about 1 hour and 15 minutes longer. 6 servings.

Mrs. Ira West, Atlanta, Georgia

WEST VIRGINIA BARBECUED CHICKEN

1/2 c. butter
1/2 clove of garlic, minced
2 tsp. flour
1/3 c. water
3 tbsp. lemon juice
3 tsp. sugar

2 tsp. salt
1/8 tsp. pepper
1/8 tsp. hot sauce
1/4 tsp. thyme
2 2 1/2-lb. broilers, halved

Melt the butter in a saucepan over low heat and add garlic. Stir in the flour and cook until bubbly. Stir in remaining ingredients except broiler halves and cook over low heat, stirring constantly, until smooth and thickened. Brush on both sides of chickens and place chickens on grill over coals. Cook for about 1 hour, turning every 15 minutes and brush frequently with sauce. 4 servings.

Mrs. Ramsey Campbell, Morgantown, West Virginia

FRICASSEED CHICKEN

1 c. flour
Salt and pepper to taste
Paprika to taste
1 fryer, disjointed
1/2 c. shortening
1/2 c. butter

1/2 c. minced onion
1/2 c. chopped celery with
  leaves
1/2 c. chopped green pepper
1 can cream of mushroom soup
1 soup can water

Place the flour, salt, pepper and paprika in a large paper bag. Add the chicken, several pieces at a time, and shake until coated. Melt the shortening and butter in a frying pan. Add the chicken and brown well on both sides. Remove from frying pan. Pour off all fat except 1/4 cup. Saute the onion, celery and green pepper in the fat in the frying pan until tender. Add the chicken. Mix the soup and water and pour over chicken. Cover frying pan. Simmer for 35 to 40 minutes and serve over rice, buttered noodles or grits. 6 servings.

Mrs. R. A. Brush, Faber, Virginia

Prune-Chicken Cacciatore (below)

PRUNE-CHICKEN CACCIATORE

1/2 c. flour	1 c. chopped onions
1 tsp. salt	1 tbsp. chopped parsley
1/4 tsp. pepper	1 1-lb. can tomatoes
1 3 1/2-lb. fryer, disjointed	1/4 c. wine or water
3 tbsp. oil	1/2 c. pitted California prunes,
1 clove of garlic, minced	halved

Mix the flour, salt and pepper and coat chicken with seasoned flour. Brown in oil in a large skillet, then add remaining ingredients. Bring to a boil and cover. Simmer for 45 minutes to 1 hour or until chicken is tender. 4 servings.

GARLIC-FRIED CHICKEN

2 2 1/2-lb. fryers, disjointed	1/2 tsp. salt
1 c. sour cream	1/4 tsp. pepper
2 tbsp. lemon juice	1/4 tsp. celery salt
1 tsp. Worcestershire sauce	1/2 tsp. paprika
1 clove of garlic, grated	Flour

Place the chicken in a shallow dish. Mix remaining ingredients except flour and spread over chicken. Cover and refrigerate overnight. Drain chicken and dredge with flour. Fry in small amount of fat in a skillet until done. 6 servings.

Mrs. Jim Hudson, Celeste, Texas

BOUCLE CHICKEN

1 pkg. onion soup mix	1 c. evaporated milk
1 fryer, disjointed	1 c. flour
Salt and pepper to taste	

Place the soup mix in a plastic bag and roll with a rolling pin until fine. Season the chicken with salt and pepper and dip into milk. Add the flour to soup mix and shake chicken in plastic bag until coated. Fry in deep, hot fat until golden brown and tender.

Mrs. Roland Pendergrass, Tomahawk, North Carolina

CHICKEN CHEVRON

1 c. pancake mix	2 eggs, well beaten
Chicken pieces	Paprika to taste
Salt to taste	1 c. corn flake crumbs

Place the pancake mix in a paper bag. Sprinkle the chicken with salt and place in pancake mix. Shake until coated. Dip chicken in egg and sprinkle with paprika. Roll in corn flake crumbs. Fry in deep, hot fat for about 20 minutes. Serve with rice.

Mrs. Joe H. Nuchols, Dumas, Arkansas

FRIED CHICKEN DELUXE

1 fryer, disjointed	1 1/2 c. milk
Salt and pepper to taste	1 egg, beaten
2 c. flour	3 c. finely crushed crackers

Season the chicken with salt and pepper and roll in flour. Mix the milk and egg in a bowl and dip chicken in milk mixture. Roll in cracker crumbs. Cook in deep, hot fat until brown and tender.

Mrs. Dorothy Robertson, Saltillo, Tennessee

LAN-DO FRIED CHICKEN

1 egg, beaten	Salt and pepper to taste
1/2 c. buttermilk	Paprika
1 chicken, disjointed	Vegetable shortening
1 c. flour	

Mix the egg and buttermilk and dip chicken in egg mixture. Place the flour in a paper bag. Add the chicken and shake until coated. Season with salt and pepper and sprinkle liberally with paprika. Cook in a skillet in 1/2 inch hot shortening until tender and golden brown.

Mrs. Clayton Duncan, Gravette, Arkansas

> **Flavor Boost for Frozen or Forgotten Chicken**
> To improve the flavor of poultry stored too long in the refrigerator or freezer, soak for 1 to 2 hours in a mixture of 1 quart cold water and 2 tablespoons baking soda.

OLD-TIME HERBED FRIED CHICKEN

1/2 c. all-purpose flour	1/8 tsp. thyme
1 tbsp. salt	1 3 lb. fryer, disjointed
1/2 tsp. pepper	Butter

Combine the flour and seasonings in a bowl and coat chicken with the flour mixture. Place in a skillet in 1 inch hot butter and cover. Cook over low heat for 15 minutes. Uncover and cook, turning, until golden brown. 4 servings.

Hazel Wimer, Hightown, Virginia

SOUTHERN OVEN-FRIED CHICKEN

1 4-oz. package potato chips	1 2 1/2 to 3-lb. fryer
1/4 tsp. garlic salt	1/3 c. melted butter or
Dash of pepper	margarine

Crush the potato chips and place in a bowl. Add the garlic salt and pepper and mix well. Cut the chicken in serving pieces and dip in butter. Roll in potato chip mixture and place, skin side up, in single layer in greased jelly roll pan. Bake at 375 degrees for 1 hour or until tender. 4 servings.

Mrs. H. E. Peterson, Louisville, Kentucky

> **Freeze-Ahead Chicken Dinners**
> Take advantage of specially priced chicken offers: plan to freeze family-sized servings. Cut 5 or 6 chickens into serving pieces and arrange on trays 1/2 inch apart; quick-freeze. When firm, distribute your family's favorite pieces for each meal into large plastic bags; store in freezer until needed. The remaining pieces may be preserved in an extra-large plastic bag to be stewed at a later time for use in salads, soups, etc.

SUCCULENT CHICKEN

1 lge. fryer	1 c. buttermilk
Salt and pepper to taste	1 c. flour
1 tsp. garlic salt (opt.)	2 c. corn oil or 1 c. shortening

Cut the chicken in serving pieces and sprinkle with salt, pepper, and garlic salt. Dip in buttermilk. Place in a paper bag with flour and shake until coated. Heat the oil in a skillet. Add the chicken and cook until golden brown, turning once. Drain on paper towels. Place on a platter and garnish with parsley, if desired.

Mary Y. Thompson, Ashland, Alabama

PARFAIT CHICKEN PIE

1 3-lb. fryer	1 stick margarine
1 recipe biscuit dough	Salt and pepper to taste
1 c. milk	1 recipe pie pastry
6 hard-boiled eggs, sliced	

Cook the chicken in boiling, salted water until tender. Drain and reserve broth. Roll the biscuit dough out thin on a floured surface and cut in strips. Pour reserved broth into a saucepan and add the milk. Bring to a boil. Add dumplings and cook, covered, for 5 minutes. Place the chicken and eggs in casserole and dot with 3/4 of the margarine. Add the dumplings, broth and salt and pepper. Place crust on top and brush with remaining melted margarine. Bake in 400-degree oven until brown.

Mrs. Frank Baccus, Monroe, Georgia

BAKED CHICKEN PIE

3 c. cubed cooked chicken	1 1/3 c. real mayonnaise
1 c. chopped celery	2/3 c. light cream
1 5-oz. can water chestnuts,	1/2 tsp. salt
sliced (opt.)	Dash of pepper
1/2 c. chopped onion	6 to 8 brown-and-serve rolls
1/2 c. finely shredded Cheddar	Melted margarine
cheese	

Mix the chicken, celery, water chestnuts, onion, cheese, mayonnaise, cream, salt and pepper in a medium saucepan. Stir over low heat for 4 to 6 minutes or until just warm, then spoon into a 1 1/2-quart casserole. Brush tops and sides of rolls with margarine and place on chicken mixture. Bake in 450-degree oven for 6 to 8 minutes or until rolls are golden brown. 3-4 servings.

Baked Chicken Pie (above)

CORN PATCH CHICKEN PIE

6 tbsp. butter or chicken fat	1 1/2 c. chicken broth
6 tbsp. flour	1 c. cream
1 tsp. salt	2 c. diced cooked chicken
1/4 tsp. pepper	

Melt the butter in a saucepan and stir in flour, salt and pepper. Add the chicken broth and cream and cook, stirring constantly, until thick. Add the chicken and place in a casserole.

Corn Bread Topping

1 c. buttermilk	1/4 c. flour
1/2 tsp. soda	2 tsp. baking powder
1 egg, slightly beaten	1 tsp. salt
1 c. cornmeal	3 tbsp. melted fat or salad oil

Mix the buttermilk and soda in a bowl and stir in the egg. Sift dry ingredients into egg mixture and stir lightly. Add the fat and stir well. Spread over chicken mixture. Bake at 450 degrees for 25 minutes or until brown.

Mrs. C. F. Dillow, Rogersville, Tennessee

CHICKEN-VEGETABLE PIE

1 No. 2 can mixed vegetables	2 c. sifted flour
1 1-lb. can chicken	3 tsp. baking powder
1 1/2 tsp. salt	1/3 c. cooking oil
1/4 tsp. pepper	2/3 c. milk

Preheat oven to 425 degrees. Drain the mixed vegetables and reserve liquid. Place mixed vegetables in a 10 x 6 x 1 1/2-inch baking pan. Remove chicken from bones and place over mixed vegetables. Combine reserved liquid, 1/2 teaspoon salt and pepper and pour over chicken. Sift the flour, baking powder and remaining salt together into a bowl. Pour oil and milk into flour mixture and stir with fork until mixture leaves side of bowl. Drop from spoon onto chicken mixture. Bake until biscuits are a golden brown. 4-6 servings.

Mrs. Fred Thomas, Kingwood, West Virginia

COBARDE POLLO PIE

2 tbsp. butter	1 boiled egg, diced
2 tbsp. flour	2 c. chopped cooked chicken
1/2 c. milk	Salt to taste
1 c. chicken broth	1 recipe pastry for 2-crust pie

Melt the butter in a saucepan and stir in the flour. Add the milk and broth and cook until thickened, stirring constantly. Remove from heat and add egg, chicken and salt. Roll out half the pastry on a floured surface and fit in 9-inch pie plate. Add the chicken mixture. Roll out remaining pastry and place on top of pie. Flute edge. Bake at 350 degrees for 35 to 40 minutes or until crust is lightly browned. 8 servings.

Mrs. A. N. Harrell, McLeansville, North Carolina

SOUTHERN CHICKEN UPSIDE-DOWN PIE

1/4 c. chicken fat	1/2 c. milk
1/2 c. flour	3 c. diced cooked chicken
3 c. chicken broth	1/2 c. sliced stuffed olives
1 tsp. salt	1 tbsp. lemon juice
Pinch of pepper and paprika	Corn Bread Batter

Melt the fat in a saucepan and stir in the flour. Add the broth, seasonings and milk and cook until thickened, stirring constantly. Add the chicken, olives and lemon juice and mix well. Place 2/3 of the mixture in a 10-inch casserole and pour Corn Bread Batter over top. Bake at 400 degrees for about 25 minutes or until corn bread is brown. Cut in wedges and serve upside down with remaining chicken mixture.

Corn Bread Batter

1 c. sifted flour	1/2 tsp. soda
1 c. cornmeal	3/4 tsp. salt
2 tbsp. sugar	3 tbsp. shortening
2 tsp. baking powder	1 c. buttermilk or sour milk

Sift the dry ingredients into a bowl and cut in shortening with a pastry blender until mixture resembles meal. Add the buttermilk and stir just until ingredients are blended.

Mrs. R. L. Haskins, Huntsville, Alabama

SUCCULENT CHICKEN PIE

1 4-lb. chicken	1 tbsp. chopped celery
4 tbsp. flour	1 tbsp. chopped pimentos
1 10-oz. can English peas, drained	Salt and pepper to taste
	1 recipe pie pastry

Place the chicken in a kettle and cover with boiling water. Cook over low heat until tender. Drain and reserve broth. Cool the chicken. Remove chicken from bones and chop. Pour the broth into the kettle and bring to a boil. Mix the flour with small amount of water and stir into the broth. Cook until thickened and add the peas, celery, pimentos, salt and pepper. Place the chicken in a deep baking dish and pour in broth mixture. Cover with pastry. Bake at 400 degrees for 30 minutes. 10 servings.

Mrs. Clint Warren, Hanceville, Alabama

Spaghetti with Turkey Mole Sauce (below)

SPAGHETTI WITH TURKEY MOLE SAUCE

1 4-oz. can green chilies, drained	1/8 tsp. ground cinnamon
1 clove of garlic	2 8-oz. cans tomato sauce
1 tbsp. slivered almonds	1/4 c. flour
1 tbsp. peanuts	3 12 1/2-oz. cans chicken broth
1 tsp. raisins	4 c. cubed cooked turkey
1 tsp. sesame seed	2 tbsp. salt
1/2 sq. semisweet chocolate, grated	4 to 6 qt. boiling water
1/8 tsp. ground cloves	1 lb. spaghetti

Blend the chilies, garlic, almonds, peanuts, raisins, sesame seed, chocolate, cloves, cinnamon and tomato sauce in an electric blender. Stir into flour in a saucepan and add the broth slowly. Cook, stirring constantly, until sauce boils for 1 minute. Add the turkey and heat through. Add salt to boiling water and add spaghetti gradually so that water continues to boil. Cook, stirring occasionally, until tender, then drain in a colander. Serve with turkey mole sauce. Garnish with parsley, if desired. The green chilies, garlic, almonds, peanuts and raisins may be minced if blender is not available. 8 servings.

CHEDDAR-TURKEY CASSEROLE

1 c. packaged precooked rice	1 can Cheddar cheese soup
2 tbsp. instant minced onion	1 c. milk
1 c. frozen green peas, thawed	1 c. crushed cheese crackers
2 c. diced cooked turkey	3 tbsp. melted butter

Prepare the rice according to package directions, adding instant minced onion to the boiling water. Fluff rice with a fork and spread in a greased 10 x 6 x

1 1/2-inch baking dish. Sprinkle with the green peas and cover with turkey. Mix the soup and milk and pour over turkey. Combine the cheese crackers and butter and sprinkle over top. Bake at 350 degrees for about 35 minutes. 4-6 servings.

Mrs. J. H. Burks, Gorgas, Alabama

CREAMED TURKEY WITH BISCUITS

1/2 c. butter	1/3 c. chopped pimento
1/2 c. flour	1 sm. onion, chopped fine
1 qt. hot broth	Salt and pepper to taste
2 c. diced cooked turkey	1 recipe unbaked biscuits
1 can cream of mushroom soup	

Melt the butter in large saucepan and stir in flour. Add the broth gradually and cook until thick, stirring constantly. Add remaining ingredients except biscuits and pour into a shallow casserole. Cover with biscuits. Bake for 10 to 12 minutes at 450 degrees. Milk may be substituted for part of the broth. 10 servings.

Mrs. L. M. McGill, Biloxi, Mississippi

FESTIVE ROAST TURKEY

1 10 to 12-lb. turkey	Butter or margarine
8 or 9 c. prepared stuffing	1/4 c. flour
Salt and pepper to taste	1/2 c. boiling water

Preheat oven to 350 degrees. Fill cavity of turkey with stuffing and truss. Place turkey on rack in a roasting pan and rub on all sides with salt and pepper. Cream 1/3 cup butter. Stir in the flour and mix until smooth. Spread on the turkey breast, legs and wings. Mix 1/2 cup butter with water and stir until melted. Reserve for basting. Roast the turkey for 4 hours or until tender, basting every 15 minutes with reserved butter mixture and turning turkey occasionally to brown on all sides. Cover with foil if turkey browns too fast.

Mrs. Ross Gutierrez, Hurst, Texas

TASTY TURKEY HASH

1/4 c. chopped onion	1 1/2 c. turkey dressing
1/4 c. diced celery	3/4 to 1 c. turkey broth or
2 tbsp. shortening	gravy
2 c. diced cooked turkey	Salt and pepper to taste

Cook the onion and celery in shortening in a saucepan until tender. Add the turkey, dressing and broth and mix well. Season with salt and pepper and heat through. 3-4 servings.

Mrs. Carl Green, Richmond, Kentucky

TURKEY CROQUETTES

3 tbsp. butter	1/2 tsp. grated onion
5 tbsp. sifted flour	1/4 tsp. salt
1 c. milk	1/8 tsp. pepper
1/4 tsp. celery salt	2 c. minced cooked turkey
1/4 tsp. lemon juice	3/4 c. bread crumbs
1/2 tsp. steak sauce	1 beaten egg

Melt the butter in a saucepan and stir in flour. Add the milk and cook until thick, stirring constantly. Add the celery salt, lemon juice, steak sauce, onion, salt and pepper and mix well. Stir in the turkey and shape in balls. Roll in crumbs. Dip into egg and roll in crumbs. Fry in deep fat until brown.

Mrs. Willis McNeely, Dublin, Georgia

TURKEY-STUFFED GREEN PEPPERS

3 lge. green peppers	Chicken bouillon or hot water
6 c. corn bread stuffing mix	2 c. chopped cooked turkey
2 eggs, beaten	Grated sharp cheese

Cut the green peppers in half lengthwise and remove seeds. Cook in boiling water for 2 to 3 minutes, then drain. Arrange, hollow side up, in a casserole. Mix the stuffing mix with eggs. Add enough bouillon to moisten and mix. Add the turkey and mix well. Fill the green peppers with turkey mixture and cover with cheese. Bake at 350 degrees for about 25 minutes. Serve with mushroom sauce, if desired. 6 servings.

Mrs. M. D. Irving, Pass Christian, Mississippi

BEST BARBECUED TURKEY

1/2 c. chopped onion	2 tsp. prepared mustard
1 1/2 tbsp. butter	1 tsp. salt
1 1/2 c. catsup	1/4 tsp. pepper
1/4 c. (packed) brown sugar	1 6 to 12-lb. fresh or
1 clove of garlic, minced	frozen turkey
1 lemon, thinly sliced	Barbecue salt or seasoning
1/4 c. Worcestershire sauce	

Saute the onion in butter in a small saucepan until lightly browned. Add remaining ingredients except turkey and barbecue salt and simmer for 20 minutes. Remove lemon slices. Store in covered jar in refrigerator if not used immediately. Thaw the turkey, if frozen. Rinse turkey and pat dry. Start the charcoal briquette fire 20 to 30 minutes before cooking turkey, allowing about 5 pounds charcoal for beginning fire. Push the burning charcoal to center as turkey cooks and fire burns and add new briquettes as needed around edge. Sprinkle cavity of the turkey generously with barbecue salt, using 2 to 3 tablespoons, then prepare turkey as for roasting, flattening wings over breast and tying securely. Insert the spit rod in front of tail and run diagonally through breast bone. Fasten tightly with spit forks at both ends and tie legs together securely with twine. Test for

best value seafoods

Years from now, scientists tell us, we will be harvesting much of our food from the sea. Southern homemakers are well ahead of these predictions: they know that when fishing boats return to Gulf and Atlantic ports laden with fish and shellfish, that's the signal to serve their families delicious, inexpensive seafood dishes.

The very best of such dishes are yours, now, with the recipes that appear in the following pages. All of us know about the famous Creole dish featuring shrimp and rice. But how many know that it can be a low-cost dish, as well? Turn to the recipe you'll find for Creole Shrimp and Rice: it's low in cost but high in flavor appeal. Another well-known southern food is oysters, and many people consider them gourmet fare. But with the recipe for Deep South Oyster Pie — and oysters bought in their season — these delicacies can form an inexpensive dish for your family, too.

There are other high-flavor recipes in this section . . . recipes like crispy Fish Fritters, elegant Perch Florentine, or hot and biting Curried Tuna on Rice. All are home-tested, family-approved recipes developed by inventive homemakers who wanted to serve the very best foods — at the lowest possible cost. And isn't that your aim, too? You can achieve it with the seafood recipes you'll find in this delightful section.

BAKED FISH AU GRATIN

1 1-lb. package frozen fish fillets	1/4 tsp. salt
2 tbsp. fine cracker crumbs	1/8 tsp. pepper
1 c. canned tomatoes	2 tbsp. margarine
2 tbsp. chopped onion	1/4 c. grated Cheddar cheese

Thaw the fillets. Sprinkle the cracker crumbs in a greased shallow 1-quart baking dish and place the fillets on crumbs. Combine the tomatoes, onion, salt and pepper and pour over fillets. Dot with margarine and sprinkle with cheese. Bake at 350 degrees for 35 minutes or until fish flakes easily when tested with a fork.

Mrs. J. T. Singer, Augusta, Georgia

Surplus Fish Storage
Empty milk cartons furnish convenient and compact storage containers for surplus fish. Place fish in cartons; fill with water, and freeze. To defrost, cut away carton and allow ice to melt in sink.

BAKED FISH FILLETS

2 lb. fish fillets	2 tbsp. flour
1/4 tsp. paprika	1 tbsp. dry mustard
3 tbsp. lemon juice	1 c. milk
Salt and pepper to taste	1/2 c. buttered bread crumbs
2 tbsp. margarine	1 tbsp. minced parsley

Cut the fillets in serving pieces and place in a greased, shallow baking dish. Sprinkle with paprika, lemon juice, salt and pepper. Melt the margarine in a saucepan and stir in the flour and mustard. Add the milk gradually and cook, stirring, until thickened. Season with salt and pepper. Pour over fillets and sprinkle with crumbs and parsley. Bake in 350-degree oven for 35 minutes. 6 servings.

Mrs. V. G. Bryson, Sr., Bassett, Virginia

FILLET TURBANS

1 tbsp. chopped onion	1/4 tsp. salt
1 tbsp. chopped celery	1/8 tsp. pepper
4 tbsp. melted margarine	1 c. fine dry bread crumbs
1/2 c. finely chopped watercress	4 fish fillets

Saute the onion and celery in 2 tablespoons margarine in a saucepan until tender, then stir in the watercress, salt, pepper and bread crumbs. Roll fillets around inside of 4 greased custard cups or muffin tins. Spoon stuffing into centers and brush with remaining margarine. Bake in 375-degree oven for 20 to 25 minutes or until fish flakes easily when tested with a fork. Turn out on a serving dish and garnish with additional watercress.

Mrs. Alton Cadenhead, Biloxi, Mississippi

BAKED FISH ROLL

2 c. flaked cooked fish
1 c. milk
3 tbsp. lemon juice
1 sm. onion, minced
1/4 c. minced parsley

Salt and pepper to taste
1 recipe biscuit dough
1 recipe white sauce
2 tbsp. minced green pepper

Mix the fish, milk, lemon juice, onion, parsley, salt and pepper. Roll the biscuit dough out on a floured board to a rectangle and spread fish mixture on dough. Roll as for jelly roll and place on a baking sheet. Bake at 425 degrees for about 30 minutes, then slice. Mix the white sauce and green pepper and serve with fish slices.

Mrs. O. T. Freeman, Attalla, Alabama

COUNTRY-STYLE FISH WITH TARTAR PEACHES

1 1-lb. 13-oz. can cling peach
   halves
2/3 c. milk
1 tbsp. instant minced onion
1 tsp. salt

2 lb. fish steaks or fillets
1/2 c. melted butter or margarine
3 c. soft bread crumbs
2 tbsp. lemon juice
1 c. tartar sauce

Drain the peach halves. Combine the milk, onion and salt. Pour over fish and let stand for 15 minutes. Pour the butter over crumbs and mix lightly. Drain the fish and arrange on a greased shallow baking pan. Top each piece with buttered crumbs. Sprinkle the lemon juice over peach halves. Fill peach cups with tartar sauce and place on baking pan with fish. Bake in 400-degree oven for 15 to 18 minutes. 4-6 servings.

Country-Style Fish with Tartar Peaches (above)

FISH FRITTERS

1 1/2 c. flour	1/4 c. milk
1 tsp. salt	1 tbsp. melted margarine
1/8 tsp. pepper	2 c. flaked cooked fish
3 eggs, beaten	

Sift the dry ingredients together into a bowl. Add the eggs and milk and mix well. Stir in the margarine and fish and drop by small spoonfuls into deep fat at 370 degrees. Fry for 3 minutes or until golden brown. Drain on absorbent paper. Serve with tartar sauce and lemon wedges, if desired.

Mrs. Ernest Nichols, Mt. Airy, North Carolina

FISH CAKES

1 lb. fish fillets	1 tbsp. mayonnaise
1 bay leaf	1 tbsp. Worcestershire sauce
Whole allspice to taste	Dash of hot sauce
Evaporated milk	1 tbsp. chopped parsley
2 slices bread	1 tsp. baking powder
1 tbsp. seafood seasoning	2 eggs, beaten
1 tsp. salt	1 tbsp. onion flakes

Place the fillets in a saucepan and add just enough water to cover. Add the bay leaf and allspice and bring to a boil. Cook for 5 minutes, then drain and cool. Flake the fish. Add enough milk to bread to moisten. Stir in the fish and remaining ingredients and shape into small cakes. Fry in small amount of fat in a skillet until brown.

Velma Niskanen, Arlington, Virginia

Basic Fried Fish (page 87)

FRIED FISH

Salt to taste	3/4 c. milk
8 pieces of fresh fish	1 egg
Pancake flour	1/4 c. lemon-lime carbonated drink

Salt the fish. Shake in a bag containing pancake flour until pieces are coated. Remove from bag and let set for 20 minutes. Mix 1 cup pancake flour with milk in a bowl. Beat egg with carbonated drink and stir into the milk mixture. Mixture should be thin. Dip fish into batter and drop into deep fat at 400 degrees. Cook for 4 to 6 minutes or until brown. Drain on absorbent paper.

Florence Bayles, Knoxville, Tennessee

GOLDEN-BAKED FISH

2 c. crushed potato chips	2 lb. fish fillets
2 tsp. paprika	1 c. evaporated milk
2 tsp. salt	2 tbsp. salad oil

Preheat oven to 400 degrees. Mix the potato chips, paprika and salt in a bowl. Cut the fillets in serving pieces and dip into the milk. Dip in potato chip mixture, coating well on all sides. Place in a greased cookie pan and drizzle salad oil over fish. Bake for 20 minutes or until fish flakes easily with fork. 6 servings.

Mrs. A. R. Metts, Lexington, Kentucky

MACKEREL CROQUETTES

1 can mackerel, drained	2 tsp. salt
2 eggs	2 tbsp. (about) flour
2 tsp. finely chopped onion	Fine cracker crumbs

Break the mackerel into small pieces. Blend 1 egg with onion, salt and flour in a bowl and shape into croquettes, using 1 heaping tablespoon for each. Beat remaining egg in a bowl and dip croquettes into egg. Roll in cracker crumbs. Fry in deep, hot fat until brown and drain on absorbent paper.

Mrs. James Rouse, Quinton, Oklahoma

BASIC FRIED FISH

1/2 c. vegetable shortening	1 tbsp. milk
1 1/2 lb. fillets of sole	3/4 to 1 c. crumbs or meal
Salt and pepper to taste	Lemon wedges
1 egg	Parsley

Heat the shortening in a large skillet. Sprinkle the fillets with salt and pepper. Beat the egg with milk and dip fillets into egg mixture. Dip in crumbs. Fry in the shortening over medium-high heat until golden brown on each side. Serve immediately with lemon wedges and garnish with parsley. Serve with tartar sauce, if desired. Cod, halibut or flounder fillets may be substituted for sole.

MACKEREL LOAF

1 can mackerel	1 tsp. salt
3/4 c. bread crumbs	1 tbsp. melted margarine
3/4 c. milk	1/2 c. chopped onion
1/2 c. pickle relish	4 slices bacon
2 eggs, beaten	

Drain the mackerel, flake and place in a bowl. Add the bread crumbs, milk, pickle relish, eggs, salt, margarine and onion and mix well. Pack in a well-greased loaf pan and place bacon on top. Bake at 350 degrees for 45 minutes, then slice.

Mrs. J. L. Jones, Blackridge, Virginia

MRS. WEAVER'S FRIED FISH

1 c. buttermilk	1/2 c. flour
Juice of 1/2 lemon	1 c. cornmeal
Fish fillets	Salt to taste

Mix the buttermilk and lemon juice and dip fish into buttermilk mixture. Mix the flour and cornmeal and roll fish in flour mixture. Fry in deep, hot fat until brown, then sprinkle with salt.

Mrs. Venice Weaver, Centre, Alabama

LAYERED FISH DISH

1 c. bread crumbs	1 tbsp. minced onion (opt.)
1 carrot, grated	1 lb. frozen ocean perch fillets,
1 stalk celery, minced	thawed
1 tsp. parsley flakes	Butter or margarine

Mix the bread crumbs, carrot, celery, parsley and onion. Place half the fillets in a greased casserole and add half the crumbs mixture. Repeat layers and dot with butter. Cover. Bake at 350 degrees for 30 minutes.

Mrs. Robert H. Pearson, Huntsville, Alabama

PERCH FLORENTINE

1 lb. frozen ocean perch fillets	Dash of nutmeg
1 10-oz. package frozen chopped	1/4 c. melted fat or oil
spinach	1 1/2 c. milk
1/4 c. flour	1/2 c. grated Parmesan cheese
1/2 tsp. salt	1/2 tsp. Worcestershire sauce
1/8 tsp. pepper	Paprika

Thaw and skin the fillets. Cook the spinach according to package directions and drain thoroughly. Blend the flour, salt, pepper and nutmeg into fat in a sauce-pan. Add milk gradually and cook until thick and smooth, stirring constantly. Add the cheese and Worcestershire sauce and stir until blended. Arrange half the fillits in a well-greased 10 x 6 x 2-inch baking dish. Combine spinach with 1/2 cup of the sauce and spread over fillets. Arrange remaining fillets over spinach mixture and top with remaining sauce. Sprinkle with paprika. Bake at 350 degrees for 25 to 30 minutes or until fish flakes easily when tested with a fork. 6 servings.

Mrs. John M. Raine, Atlanta, Georgia

SALMON AND PEAS WESTERN

1 head western iceberg lettuce	Salt to taste
1 1-lb. can salmon	Salad oil
1/4 c. sweet pickle relish	3 tbsp. butter or margarine
3 tbsp. finely chopped onion	3 tbsp. flour
1/2 c. fine dry bread crumbs	3/4 c. milk
1 14 1/2-oz. can evaporated milk	1 c. cooked peas
1 tsp. crumbled summer savory	

Core, rinse and drain the lettuce, then chill in a disposable plastic bag. Cut four 3/4-inch crosswise slices from head of lettuce. Wrap remainder in disposable plastic bag and store in refrigerator for later use. Drain the salmon and flake fine with fork. Drain the relish. Combine the salmon, relish, onion, 1/4 cup bread crumbs, 1/3 cup evaporated milk, 1/2 teaspoon savory and salt and shape into 4 rounded cones. Coat each cone with evaporated milk and roll in remaining crumbs. Brush cones with oil gently and place in a baking pan. Bake in 350-degree oven for 35 minutes. Melt the butter in a saucepan and stir in flour. Stir in remaining evaporated milk, remaining savory and the milk. Cook and stir until mixture comes to a boil and is thickened. Stir in the peas and add salt. Place sliced lettuce in a colander over boiling water and cover. Steam for 2 minutes. Transfer lettuce to serving dish and top with salmon cones and creamed peas. 4 servings.

Salmon and Peas Western (above)

89

DELICIOUS SALMON LOAF

1/4 c. milk, scalded	Juice of 1/2 lemon
3/4 c. soft bread crumbs	1/8 tsp. pepper
2 tbsp. melted margarine	1/2 tsp. salt
1 1-lb. can salmon	1 tsp. minced parsley
2 eggs, separated	1/2 tsp. onion juice

Mix the milk and bread crumbs in a bowl and stir in the margarine. Drain the salmon and remove skin and bones. Add salmon to the milk mixture, then stir in the egg yolks, lemon juice, pepper, salt, parsley and onion juice. Fold in stiffly beaten egg whites and place in a well-greased loaf pan. Bake at 375 degrees for about 35 minutes. 4-5 servings.

Mrs. Henry Sadler, Columbia, South Carolina

FISH SHELL BAKE

1 1/2 c. shell macaroni	1 c. milk
1 8-oz. can pink salmon	1 tsp. salt
2 tbsp. margarine	2 tsp. lemon juice
1/4 c. finely chopped onion	2 tbsp. minced parsley
2 tbsp. flour	1 c. grated cheese

Cook the macaroni according to package directions. Drain the salmon and break into small pieces. Melt the margarine in a saucepan. Add onion and cook until tender. Blend in the flour. Add the milk slowly, constantly stirring and cook until thickened. Stir in the salt, lemon juice and parsley. Arrange alternate layers of macaroni, salmon and cheese in a greased 1 1/2-quart casserole and pour sauce over top. Bake at 350 degrees for about 30 minutes or until heated through.

Mrs. Cullen Payne, Loraine, Texas

SALMON-NOODLE RING

2 tbsp. melted margarine	Salt and pepper to taste
1 tbsp. flour	2 c. cooked seasoned noodles
1 c. milk	1 c. buttered bread crumbs
2 c. flaked red salmon	

Combine the margarine and flour in a saucepan. Add the milk and cook, stirring constantly, until thickened and smooth. Add the salmon, salt and pepper and mix well. Place alternate layers of salmon mixture, noodles and crumbs in a well-greased ring mold. Bake at 375 degrees for 20 to 30 minutes. Unmold. Center may be filled with buttered cooked peas and carrots. Garnish with slices of hard-cooked eggs. 8 servings.

Mrs. John R. Evanson, Judsonia, Arkansas

RICE-SALMON LOAF

1 1-lb. can salmon	2 tsp. salt
2 c. cooked rice	1 tsp. pepper
1 tbsp. lemon juice	5 tbsp. melted margarine

| 2 eggs, beaten | 2 tbsp. flour |
| 1/3 c. bread crumbs | 1 c. milk |

Remove bones from the salmon and place the salmon and liquid in a bowl. Break the salmon into small pieces. Add the rice, lemon juice, 1 teaspoon salt, pepper, 3 tablespoons margarine, eggs and bread crumbs and mix well. Place in a well-greased loaf pan. Bake at 350 degrees for 45 minutes. Place remaining margarine in top of a double boiler and stir in flour and remaining salt. Stir in milk and cook over boiling water until smooth and thick. Serve with the salmon mixture.

Martha Hallaway, Happy, Texas

SALMON CROQUETTES

3 tbsp. margarine	2 c. flaked salmon
4 tbsp. flour	1 tsp. minced parsley
1/2 tsp. salt	1 egg, beaten
1/8 tsp. pepper	2 tbsp. water
1 c. milk	Fine bread or cracker crumbs
1 slice onion	

Melt the margarine in a saucepan and blend in the flour, salt and pepper. Add the milk and onion and cook until thickened, stirring constantly. Cool and remove onion. Stir in the salmon and parsley and chill for 2 to 3 hours. Shape into patties. Mix the egg and water. Dip salmon patties into egg mixture, then roll in crumbs. Let set for 30 minutes. Fry in deep, hot fat until brown.

Ellen Webb Massengill, Seminole, Texas

Grocery Shopping Efficiency

Careful preparation of a grocery shopping list, including both the amounts and types of food items, is an aid in controlling impulse buying. Group similar items together, in the order found on grocery shelves.

SALMON-CHEESE PATTIES

1 1-lb. can salmon	1/8 tsp. hot sauce
1 egg, beaten	1/4 tsp. salt
3 slices bread, crumbled	1/4 tsp. pepper
1 med. onion, chopped	1 c. shredded Cheddar cheese
1/4 tsp. Worcestershire sauce	1/4 c. margarine

Drain and flake the salmon. Add remaining ingredients except margarine and mix well. Shape into patties. Melt the margarine in a large, heavy skillet. Add patties and brown on both sides.

Mrs. B. G. Buchanan, Danville, Virginia

Tuna Polynesia (below)

TUNA POLYNESIA

1 2-oz. can sliced mushrooms, drained	1 can cream of celery soup
1/2 c. green onion, cut in 1-in. pieces	1/3 c. water
2 tbsp. butter or margarine	1 7-oz. can tuna
	1/2 c. pineapple tidbits
	Cooked rice or Chinese noodles

Cook the mushrooms and onion in butter in a saucepan until tender. Blend in the soup and water. Drain and flake the tuna and add to soup mixture. Add pineapple and heat through, stirring occasionally. Serve over rice. 3 servings.

SPAGHETTI ALLA CARRETTIERA

2 tbsp. butter or margarine	1/4 c. prepared yellow mustard
2 tbsp. flour	2 7-oz. cans tuna, drained
1/2 tsp. salt	8 oz. spaghetti
2 c. milk	2 tbsp. grated Parmesan cheese

Melt the butter in a medium saucepan and blend in the flour and salt. Stir in the milk gradually. Bring to a boil and cook, stirring occasionally, until thickened. Stir in the mustard and tuna. Cook the spaghetti according to package directions. Place in a serving dish and sprinkle with cheese. Serve tuna mixture over spaghetti. 4 servings.

Photograph for this recipe on page 82.

CALCUTTA TUNA PATTIES

1 7-oz. can tuna, flaked	1/2 tsp. curry powder
2 c. mashed potatoes	2 tbsp. flour
1 sm. onion, minced	Salt and pepper to taste
1 egg	3 tbsp. shortening

Combine all ingredients except the shortening in a bowl and mix well. Shape into patties. Fry in hot shortening in a skillet until browned on both sides. Drain on absorbent paper. 6 servings.

Mrs. Thelma Olson, Lexington, Oklahoma

COMPANY TUNA

1 lge. onion, chopped	1/2 c. warm water
3 stalks celery, chopped	1 lge. can grated tuna, drained
Oregano to taste	Salt and pepper to taste
1 can Cheddar cheese soup	8 crumbled oblong buttery crackers

Saute the onion and celery in small amount of fat in a saucepan until tender. Sprinkle with oregano and mix well. Stir in the soup and water. Add tuna, salt and pepper and mix. Pour into a 2-quart casserole and top with cracker crumbs. Bake at 325 degrees for 45 minutes to 1 hour or until browned. 4-6 servings.

Mrs. Waldron B. Rodgers, Brevard, North Carolina

CREAM TUNA ON TOAST

4 tbsp. margarine or butter	2 7-oz. cans chunk tuna
4 tbsp. flour	9 pieces of toast
2 1/2 c. milk	

Melt the margarine in a skillet and blend in flour. Add the milk gradually and cook, stirring constantly, until thickened. Add the tuna and heat through. Serve on toast.

Mrs. Charles Thorn, Dobbin, Texas

CURRIED TUNA AND RICE

1 lge. onion, chopped	1/2 c. seedless raisins
4 tbsp. margarine	Salt to taste
4 tbsp. flour	2 7-oz. cans tuna
2 tsp. curry powder	3 c. buttered cooked rice
2 c. milk	

Brown the onion lightly in margarine in a saucepan and blend in flour and curry powder. Add the milk and cook, stirring, until thick. Add the raisins and salt. Drain the tuna and break into bite-sized pieces. Add to sauce and heat through. Serve over rice. 6-8 servings.

Mrs. H. L. Peterson, Birmingham, Alabama

RICE AND TUNA

3 tbsp. butter or margarine	1 7-oz. can tuna
3 tbsp. flour	2 c. cooked rice
2 c. milk	1/4 c. chopped parsley
1/2 tsp. salt	1 c. high protein cereal
1/2 tsp. paprika	1 tsp. melted butter or margarine
2 c. grated Cheddar cheese	

Melt the butter in a saucepan and stir in flour. Add milk gradually and cook until thickened, stirring constantly. Add the salt, paprika and cheese and stir until cheese has melted. Drain and flake the tuna. Place alternate layers of rice, tuna, parsley and cheese sauce in greased 1 1/2-quart casserole. Crush the cereal and combine with melted butter. Sprinkle over tuna mixture. Bake in 400-degree oven for 25 minutes or until heated through.

Mrs. C. V. Cherry, Spencer, Oklahoma

TUNA-CORN BREAD PIE

12 thin lemon slices	2 eggs, beaten
1 6 1/2 or 7-oz. can tuna	1 can cream of mushroom soup
1/2 c. fresh bread crumbs	1 pkg. corn muffin mix
2 tbsp. minced onion	

Preheat oven to 400 degrees. Arrange lemon slices on bottom of lightly greased 10-inch pie plate. Drain and flake the tuna and blend with bread crumbs, onion, eggs and soup. Spoon into pie plate over lemon slices. Prepare corn muffin mix according to package directions and spoon over tuna mixture. Bake for 30 minutes or until golden brown. Cool for 10 minutes. Loosen sides of pie with a spatula. Invert serving dish on top of pie plate and invert both, unmolding pie bottom side up. Garnish with parsley. 6 servings.

Mrs. Robert P. Quinn, Houston, Texas

Time-Saving Tuna Tip
Although brine-packed tuna is lower in calories, it is also more expensive. The oil-packed variety may be rinsed and drained before use. Moreover, oil-packed tuna is available in low-cost flakes rather than expensive chunks or pieces found in water-packed varieties.

DEEP-SOUTH OYSTER PIES

Pastry for 2-crust pie	1/2 tsp. salt
1 can cream of celery soup	Pinch of pepper
3 c. diced potatoes	1 tbsp. margarine
2 tbsp. cornstarch	1 tbsp. dried parsley
1 pt. standard oysters	Melted margarine

Line 4 individual pie pans or casseroles with pastry. Pour the celery soup into a saucepan. Add the potatoes and simmer until potatoes are tender. Mix the cornstarch with a small amount of water. Stir into the potato mixture and cook until thick. Add oysters with liquid. Add more cornstarch if not thick enough. Add the seasonings, margarine and parsley and bring to a boil. Pour into pie pans. Add top crusts and seal edges with a fork. Cut slits in centers of crusts and brush crusts with melted margarine. Bake in 400-degree oven until brown.

Betty Neff Dickens, Ft. Lauderdale, Florida

OYSTER-TUNA SURPRISE

2 cans frozen oyster stew	2 6 1/2-oz. cans chunk tuna
1 1 1/2-lb. package frozen stew vegetables	1 10-oz. package frozen peas
2 tbsp. flour	1 tbsp. Worcestershire sauce
1/3 c. water	1/2 c. sour cream

Place the oyster stew in a 2-quart saucepan and cook over low heat, stirring occasionally, until completely thawed. Cook the stew vegetables in another saucepan according to package directions and drain. Remove oysters from stew and set aside. Blend the flour with water until smooth, add to oyster stew and cook, stirring constantly, until smooth and thickened. Add the stew vegetables. Drain and rinse the tuna and add to vegetable mixture. Add the peas and cook over low heat for about 5 minutes or until peas are tender-crisp. Stir in the Worcestershire sauce, sour cream and the reserved oysters and heat just to the boiling point. Remove from heat and serve immediately. 6-8 servings.

Oyster-Tuna Surprise (above)

OYSTER-MACARONI WITH CHEESE

1/2 c. chopped onion	1 7-oz. package elbow macaroni
2 tbsp. margarine	2 tbsp. chopped green pepper
2 10 1/2-oz. cans oyster stew	1 1/2 c. shredded Cheddar cheese

Saute the onion in margarine in a saucepan. Add the oyster stew, macaroni and green pepper and cover. Cook over low heat, stirring occasionally, until macaroni is tender. Stir in the cheese and stir until cheese melts. 4-6 servings.

Patricia Burge, Batesville, Arkansas

BAKED CORN AND OYSTERS

1 No. 2 can corn	1 tsp. pepper
1 c. crushed crackers	1 tsp. sugar
1 egg, beaten	1/4 c. melted margarine
1 tsp. salt	1 c. small fresh oysters
1/2 c. milk	

Combine all ingredients in order listed and place in a greased baking dish. Bake at 375 degrees for 25 minutes. Do not overbake.

Mrs. Ella M. Burgess, Mannsville, Oklahoma

BAKED SHRIMP DISH

1 can shrimp, drained	1/2 c. mayonnaise
1/2 c. chopped celery	1 can mushroom soup
1/2 c. chopped bell pepper	2 tsp. Worcestershire sauce
1 1/2 c. cooked rice	1/2 c. grated cheese
1/2 c. water	1/2 c. buttered crumbs

Mix all ingredients except cheese and crumbs and place in a 2-quart casserole. Bake at 350 degrees for 20 minutes. Top with cheese and crumbs and bake until brown.

Mrs. L. B. Whaley, Webb, Alabama

SHRIMP AND CORN PIE

2 c. fresh cut corn	1 c. cooked shrimp
2 eggs, slightly beaten	1 tsp. Worcestershire sauce
1 tbsp. margarine	Salt and pepper to taste
1/2 c. milk	Mace to taste

Combine all ingredients in order listed and place in a greased shallow baking dish. Place in pan of hot water. Bake at 350 degrees for 30 minutes or until firm. One 17-ounce can cream-style corn may be substituted for fresh corn. 4 servings.

Mrs. Milton Angelakos, Dublin, Georgia

CREOLE SHRIMP AND RICE

1 c. diced celery
3 sm. cloves of garlic, minced
1 c. chopped onion
1/2 c. chopped bell pepper
1 stick margarine
1/2 c. chopped green onion tops
1 can cream of mushroom soup
1 can tomato soup
6 sprigs of parsley, chopped
1 lb. cooked cleaned shrimp
3 slices bread, moistened
3 c. cooked rice
Salt and pepper to taste
1/4 c. bread crumbs
1/4 c. grated Parmesan cheese

Saute the celery, garlic, onion and bell pepper in margarine in a saucepan until tender. Add the green onion tops, soups, parsley and shrimp and cook over low heat for 5 minutes. Add bread and rice and cook for 15 minutes longer. Add the salt and pepper. Turn into 2-quart casserole and sprinkle with bread crumbs and cheese. Cover. Bake in 375-degree oven for 30 minutes. Uncover and bake for 5 minutes longer. 8 servings.

Mrs. Ann Hanks, Duson, Louisiana

SHRIMP-RICE PARTY CASSEROLE

1 1/2 lb. cleaned fresh shrimp, chopped
1/2 c. chopped green pepper
1/2 c. chopped onions
2 cloves of garlic, crushed
2 tbsp. vegetable oil
1 4-oz. can sliced mushrooms, drained
3 c. cooked rice
1 1/2 tsp. salt
1/4 tsp. pepper
1/2 c. tomato juice

Saute the shrimp, green pepper, onions and garlic in the oil in a skillet until vegetables are tender but not brown. Stir in remaining ingredients and place in a casserole. Bake at 375 degrees for 25 minutes or until heated through. 6 servings.

Shrimp-Rice Party Casserole (above)

SHRIMP AND MACARONI PIE

1/2 lb. elbow macaroni	Salt and pepper to taste
2 tbsp. butter or margarine	2 c. small cooked shrimp
1 c. grated sharp cheese	2 c. milk
1 tsp. prepared mustard	3 eggs, slightly beaten

Cook the macaroni according to package directions and drain. Add the butter and mix well. Add the cheese, mustard, salt, pepper and shrimp and mix well. Turn into a greased 2-quart casserole. Mix the milk and eggs and pour over shrimp mixture. Bake at 325 degrees for 30 to 35 minutes.

Mrs. Eva G. Key, Mount Pleasant, South Carolina

SHRIMP AND RICE

1/2 lb. shrimp	4 slices bacon, chopped
1 tsp. sugar	3 c. cooked rice
Dash of pepper	1 egg, beaten
Soy sauce	2 green onions, chopped
1 clove of garlic, chopped	

Peel and clean shrimp and cut into small pieces. Place in a bowl and sprinkle with sugar, pepper and 1 tablespoon soy sauce. Let stand for 20 minutes. Brown the garlic and bacon in a frying pan. Add the shrimp and 1 cup water and cook until shrimp are pink and liquid has evaporated, stirring frequently. Stir in the rice, egg, onions and soy sauce to taste and cook for about 5 minutes, stirring frequently. 4 servings.

Mrs. Dallas Cook, Cadiz, Kentucky

DEVILED TWINS

1 6 1/2-oz. can tuna, flaked	1 tsp. Worcestershire sauce
1 7-oz. can shrimp, drained	1/2 tsp. salt
1/2 c. minced green pepper	1/8 tsp. pepper
3/4 c. minced celery	3/4 c. salad dressing
1 tsp. finely chopped onion	1 c. soft bread crumbs
1 tbsp. prepared mustard	2 tbsp. melted margarine

Combine the tuna, shrimp, green pepper, celery, onion, mustard, Worcestershire sauce, seasonings and salad dressing and toss until well blended. Place in 4 to 6 baking shells. Mix the crumbs with the margarine and sprinkle over tuna mixture. Bake in a 350-degree oven for about 30 minutes. Garnish with lemon wedges and parsley.

Mrs. Otha Salter, Mobile, Alabama

SEAFOOD DIVINE

3 hard-cooked eggs, sliced	1 c. diced American cheese
1 c. flaked tuna	4 tbsp. margarine
1 c. shrimp	4 tbsp. flour

1 tsp. salt
Pepper to taste
2 c. milk

1 c. dry bread crumbs
1/4 c. melted margarine

Arrange the eggs in a greased casserole and cover with tuna and shrimp. Add the cheese. Melt the margarine in a saucepan and stir in the flour, salt and pepper. Add the milk and cook, stirring, until thickened. Pour over cheese. Mix the bread crumbs and melted margarine and sprinkle over white sauce. Bake in a 325-degree oven for 35 minutes.

Mrs. E. L. Ramsey, Greensboro, North Carolina

ROE PATTIES WITH SHRIMP SAUCE

1 can cod roe
1 egg, slightly beaten
Bread crumbs

2 tbsp. butter or margarine
1 can frozen shrimp soup

Open the cod roe can at both ends and press onto a plate. Cut in 1-inch slices and dip each slice in egg, then in bread crumbs. Fry in the butter in a skillet until golden brown and place on a platter. Heat the soup in a saucepan over low heat until heated through, stirring frequently. Spread over the roe patties. Garnish with dill sprigs and lemon wedges.

Roe Patties with Shrimp Sauce (above)

Cranberry-Baked Beans (page 102)

money-saving vegetables

Gleaming purple eggplant . . . golden ears of corn . . . potatoes with the damp earth of the field still on them . . . bright green and yellow beans . . . the sight of beautiful vegetables. Yes, fresh, frozen, or canned vegetables are a joy to look at. Best of all, they are low in price almost year-round – a bargain for thrifty homemakers!

Wise homemakers from Maryland to Texas know that buying vegetables in season is a good way to save food dollars. And they also know the importance of preparing nutrition-packed vegetables in flavorful, eye-appealing dishes to please their families. Over the years, these women have developed a wide range of low-cost vegetable recipes – and the best of them are shared with you now in the section which follows.

There are such purely southern dishes as Collards and Cornmeal Dumplings and Southern Okra. The first features greens and corn, and the second, okra. All are vegetables certain to appear on virtually every southern table. There are also party-elegant vegetable dishes, like Venetian Rice and Peas, Luncheon Spinach, or Scalloped Tomatoes with Onions.

You'll enjoy browsing through the pages of this section and discovering the recipes southern women use to prepare vegetables. These are recipes certain to bring requests for "more, please" . . . without straining the food budget!

BAKED BEANS

1 lge. can pork and beans	1/2 tsp. dry mustard
3 tbsp. finely chopped onion	3 tbsp. brown sugar
2 tbsp. finely chopped green	1/2 c. water
pepper	1/2 c. catsup
1 tbsp. finely chopped celery	Bacon slices

Mix all ingredients except bacon in a casserole, then cover with bacon slices. Bake in 350-degree oven for about 1 hour or until bacon is crisp and beans lightly browned.

Joe Freeman, Stuttgart, Arkansas

CRANBERRY-BAKED BEANS

1 1/2 c. dried pea beans	1 tsp. dry mustard
1 1/2 tsp. salt	1/8 tsp. ginger
2 c. cranberry juice cocktail	1/4 c. catsup
2 c. water	2 tbsp. (firmly packed) dark
1/3 c. chopped onion	brown sugar
2 tbsp. molasses	1/4 lb. salt pork, sliced

Place the beans, salt, cranberry juice and water in a saucepan and bring to a boil. Remove from heat and set aside for 1 hour. Bring to a boil and cover. Reduce heat and simmer until beans are tender, adding water if necessary. Drain and reserve liquid. Combine the beans and remaining ingredients except salt pork and pour half the mixture into a bean pot or 2-quart casserole. Top with half the salt pork, then repeat layers. Add 1 1/2 cups reserved bean liquid and cover. Bake at 250 degrees for 5 to 7 hours. Uncover and bake for 1 hour longer, adding more reserved liquid, if necessary, to keep beans from drying. Kidney, lima or marrow beans may be substituted for pea beans. 6-8 servings.

Photograph for this recipe on page 100.

CREOLE LIMAS

2 slices bacon, diced	1 1-lb. can tomatoes
1/3 c. chopped onion	1/2 tsp. salt
1/4 c. chopped green pepper	Dash of pepper
1 10-oz. package frozen lima	2 tsp. molasses
beans	

Fry the bacon in a skillet until crisp, then remove from skillet. Saute the onion and green pepper in bacon drippings in the skillet until tender. Cook the beans according to package directions and add to onion mixture. Add remaining ingredients and mix well. Simmer for 5 minutes. Serve topped with bacon. 6 servings.

Emilie Rae Fallstrom, Newport News, Virginia

DECEMBER BEANS WITH MIXED HERB BUTTER

1 lb. green beans	2 tbsp. sesame seed
1/4 c. butter or margarine	1/4 tsp. rosemary
3/4 c. minced onions	1/4 tsp. dried basil
1 clove of garlic, minced	3/4 tsp. salt
1/4 c. minced celery	1/2 c. snipped parsley

Wash and trim the beans and cut crosswise in small, slanted slices. Place in a saucepan and add 1/2 inch boiling, salted water. Cover and cook for 15 minutes or until tender. Drain. Melt the butter in a saucepan. Add the onions, garlic, celery and sesame seed and saute for 5 minutes. Add remaining ingredients and cover. Simmer for 10 minutes. Add to beans and toss well. 4 servings.

Jo Anna Littrel, Fort Meyers Beach, Florida

FAR EASTERN FRESH POLE BEANS

2 lb. fresh pole beans	1 tbsp. cornstarch
1 tbsp. olive oil	2 tbsp. cold water
1 c. chicken broth	Salt to taste

Cook the beans in boiling water until partially done, then drain well. Heat the oil in a frying pan. Add the beans and cook, stirring, until heated through. Add the broth and cover. Steam over high heat for 3 minutes. Combine the cornstarch and cold water. Push beans to side of frying pan. Add the cornstarch mixture to broth and cook, stirring, until beans are glazed and broth is slightly thickened. Add salt. Garnish with browned sweet and sour pork.

Far Eastern Fresh Pole Beans (above), Glazed Orange Peel (page 148)

KENTUCKY BEANS

4 c. dried navy beans	Salt to taste
4 tbsp. molasses	1/2 lb. salt pork, sliced
1 tsp. mustard	

Wash the beans and place in a saucepan. Add enough water to cover and soak overnight. Bring to a boil and cook for 30 minutes. Drain and place in a bean pot. Dissolve the molasses, mustard and salt in 1 cup hot water and pour over the beans. Cover. Bake at 300 degrees for 6 to 8 hours, adding water, as needed. Remove cover and place salt pork over top. Bake until pork is brown.

Mrs. Delbert Adams, Salt Lick, Kentucky

PASTA E FAGIOLI

1 onion, chopped	1 c. elbow macaroni
1 green pepper, chopped	1 can kidney beans
1 clove of garlic, chopped	1/2 c. grated Parmesan cheese
1/4 c. olive oil	

Saute the onion, green pepper and garlic in olive oil in a saucepan until tender. Cook the macaroni according to package directions and drain. Add kidney beans and onion mixture and place in a casserole. Cover with cheese. Bake at 350 degrees until browned. 6-8 servings.

Mrs. P. T. Dix Arnold, Gainesville, Florida

Year-Round, Seasonal Green Peppers
When green peppers are in season buy a plentiful supply. Chop; freeze in plastic bags. Crush the bag in order to remove the desired quantity.

GINGERED CARROTS

2 lb. carrots	6 tbsp. melted butter
2 c. water	1 tsp. ground ginger
1 1/4 tsp. salt	Pepper to taste

Peel and slice the carrots and place in a heavy saucepan. Add the water and 3/4 teaspoon salt and bring to a boil. Reduce heat and cover. Cook for 20 to 25 minutes or until tender. Remove from heat and drain. Mash carrots until smooth and add the butter, ginger, remaining salt and pepper. Cook over low heat until heated through.

Barbara Mims, Paris, Texas

BAKED SHREDDED CARROTS

1/3 c. minced onion	2 tbsp. chopped parsley
2 tbsp. margarine	3/4 tsp. salt
2 c. shredded carrots	3 tbsp. evaporated milk

Saute the onion in margarine in a saucepan until light brown. Stir in the carrots, parsley and salt and place in a well-greased baking dish. Add the milk and cover. Bake in 375-degree oven for about 30 minutes.

Mrs. Ruth Lackin, Leitchfield, Kentucky

SUNDAY SUPPER RING

1 qt. fresh Brussels sprouts	1/8 tsp. pepper
1 1/4 tsp. salt	Cheesed Noodle Ring
3 tbsp. butter or margarine	

Wash and trim the Brussels sprouts. Rinse and place in a saucepan containing 1 inch boiling water and salt. Bring to a boil and cook for 5 minutes. Cover and cook for 15 minutes longer or until Brussels sprouts are crisp-tender. Drain. Add the butter and pepper and toss lightly. Place in center of Cheesed Noodle Ring. 6 servings.

Cheesed Noodle Ring

1 lb. noodles	2 c. shredded Cheddar cheese
3 tbsp. butter	1 1/2 tsp. Worcestershire sauce

Cook the noodles in boiling, salted water until tender, then drain. Add the butter and toss until butter is melted. Pour into a well-greased ring mold and place mold in a pan of hot water. Bake at 350 degrees for 25 minutes. Unmold onto a serving plate. Melt the cheese in a double boiler and stir in the Worcestershire sauce. Pour over noodle ring.

Sunday Supper Ring (above)

105

EGG-TOPPED CARROT CASSEROLE

1 bag carrots, sliced	1 tbsp. chopped onion
1 can cream of mushroom soup	1 tbsp. green pepper
1/2 c. cubed cheese	2 hard-cooked eggs, sliced

Cook the carrots in boiling, salted water until tender, then drain. Stir in the mushroom soup, cheese, onion and green pepper and place in a casserole. Top with eggs. Bake at 350 degrees for 30 minutes. 4 servings.

Mrs. Barbara Deane, Little Rock, Arkansas

CABBAGE CAPER

1 1/2-lb. cabbage	1 c. bread crumbs
1 can cream of chicken soup	2 tbsp. margarine
1/2 soup can milk	1/2 c. grated cheese

Chop the cabbage and place in a saucepan. Add small amount of water and cook for 10 minutes. Drain. Combine the soup and milk. Combine bread crumbs and margarine. Place alternate layers of cabbage, soup mixture and cheese in 1 1/2-quart casserole and top with buttered bread crumbs. Bake at 350 degrees for 30 minutes. 6 servings.

Betty Jeans, Meridian, Mississippi

CABBAGE WEDGE MEAL-IN-ONE

1 sm. cabbage	2 c. canned tomatoes
1 c. chopped onions	1 c. hot water
1 lb. ground beef	2 tsp. salt
1/4 c. rice	1/3 tsp. pepper

Remove tough outer leaves from the cabbage. Cut cabbage into 8 wedges and cut off part of the hard core. Place wedges in a greased casserole. Place onions, ground beef and rice between wedges. Combine the tomatoes, water and seasonings and pour over casserole. Cover. Bake at 350 degrees for 1 hour and 30 minutes. 6-8 servings.

Mrs. Harry Troop, China Grove, North Carolina

FRIED CABBAGE

1 lge. cabbage	1/4 tsp. pepper
4 slices salt pork	1 tsp. salt
1/3 pod hot pepper	

Cut the cabbage in half and remove core. Shred the cabbage. Fry the salt pork in a skillet until brown and remove from skillet. Add cabbage and remaining ingredients to the skillet and cover. Cook over low heat until cabbage is tender, stirring frequently. 6 servings.

Jacksie Fender, Asheville, North Carolina

BEETS WITH ORANGE SAUCE

1/2 c. sugar	**1 tbsp. lemon juice**
2 tsp. cornstarch	**1/4 c. orange juice**
1/2 c. water	**1 tbsp. margarine**
1 tsp. grated orange rind	**1 No. 303 can beets, drained**

Combine the sugar and cornstarch in a saucepan. Add the water and bring to a boil. Reduce heat and simmer for 15 minutes. Add orange rind, lemon juice, orange juice and margarine. Add the beets and heat through. 5 servings.

Mrs. Shirley Flynn, Hot Springs, Virginia

SAUERKRAUT WITH APPLES

4 c. drained sauerkraut	**1 tbsp. light brown sugar**
2 red apples, thinly sliced	**2 tbsp. butter or margarine**
1/2 c. apple brandy	

Combine the sauerkraut, apples, brandy, brown sugar and butter in a skillet and cover. Simmer for 5 minutes or until apples are tender. Garnish with additional apple slices and parsley, if desired. May serve with pork.

Sauerkraut with Apples (above)

107

Variation for the Baked Potato
For a different, low-calorie, low-cost garnish, heap cottage cheese and chives on steaming baked potatoes instead of sour cream and butter.

COLLARDS AND CORNMEAL DUMPLINGS

1/3 lb. salt meat	1 c. cornmeal
1 bunch collards, cleaned	2 eggs, slightly beaten
1 c. flour	1/2 c. milk
2 tsp. baking powder	2 tbsp. melted butter or
1 tsp. salt	margarine

Wash the salt meat and score to the rind. Place in a heavy saucepan and add 1 inch boiling water. Cover and cook until tender. Add the collards and cook until tender. Chop well. Sift the flour, baking powder and salt together into a bowl. Stir in cornmeal. Add the eggs, milk and butter and stir until mixed. Drop by heaping spoonfuls onto waxed paper and sprinkle with additional cornmeal. Drop dumplings into simmering collards and cover tightly. Cook over low heat for 20 minutes without lifting cover.

Mrs. Margaret Betsworth, Pensacola, Florida

BOSTON-STYLE BAKED CORN

1 tsp. dry mustard	1 sm. onion, diced
1/2 tsp. salt	2 12-oz. cans whole kernel
2 tbsp. brown sugar	corn, drained
1 c. catsup	2 or 3 slices bacon, diced

Preheat oven to 350 degrees. Combine the mustard, salt, sugar and catsup in a medium bowl. Add the onion and corn and mix thoroughly. Pour into a greased 1 1/2-quart casserole and top with bacon. Bake for 40 minutes or until bacon is crisp. 6-8 servings.

Cathie Miller, Jackson, Mississippi

CORN PUDDING CASSEROLE

3 eggs, separated	1 1/2 tsp. sugar
2/3 c. milk	1 1/2 tbsp. flour
1/8 tsp. pepper	2 tsp. chopped green pepper
1 1/2 tsp. salt	1 1-lb. can whole kernel corn

Beat the egg yolks in a bowl. Add the milk, pepper, salt, sugar, flour and green pepper and mix well. Drain the corn and stir into milk mixture. Fold in stiffly beaten egg whites and pour into a greased casserole. Place in a pan of hot water. Bake in 350-degree oven for 1 hour.

Mrs. Blanche Gregory, Vinita, Oklahoma

KENTUCKY-FRIED CORN

6 strips bacon	1 med. onion, minced
4 med. ears of white corn, scraped	1 lge. egg, beaten
	Salt and pepper to taste
2 sm. cucumbers, thinly sliced	Sugar to taste

Dice the bacon and fry in a skillet until crisp. Add the corn, cucumbers, onion, egg, salt, pepper and sugar and mix thoroughly. Fry over low heat for 30 to 45 minutes, stirring frequently. Pimento strips or green pepper slices may be added, if desired. 4-6 servings.

Mrs. Mildred Roselle, Pleasure Ridge Park, Kentucky

CAULIFLOWER-VEGETABLE DISH

1 cauliflower	2 leeks, sliced
1 pkg. frozen Brussels sprouts	2 parsnips, sliced
1 pkg. frozen green peas	Melted butter or margarine
4 carrots, sliced	Lemon juice (opt.)
5 sm. beets	

Cook the cauliflower in boiling, salted water until tender, then drain. Cook the Brussels sprouts and peas according to package directions. Cook the carrots, beets, leeks and parsnips separately in boiling, salted water until tender, then drain. Place the cauliflower in center of a serving bowl and place remaining vegetables around the cauliflower. Drizzle with butter and lemon juice. May be served with hollandaise sauce, if desired.

Cauliflower-Vegetable Dish (above)

FRIED CORN

4 lge. ears of corn	1 tsp. salt
4 slices bacon	1 tbsp. cornstarch
1 tbsp. sugar	

Cut tips from corn kernels, using sharp knife, and scrape down remaining corn to remove pulpy liquid from cobs. Cook bacon in 9-inch skillet over low heat until crisp. Drain and crumble. Drain all except 2 tablespoons bacon drippings from skillet. Stir corn, 1 1/4 cups water, sugar and salt into drippings and bring to a boil. Cover and simmer for 20 to 25 minutes, stirring occasionally. Mix cornstarch and 2 tablespoons water until smooth and stir into corn mixture. Bring to a boil and cook for 1 minute, stirring constantly. Add bacon. 4 servings.

Mrs. Taylor Orr, Covington, Kentucky

LYE HOMINY

5 qt. dried shelled white corn	6 oz. lye
	6 qt. cold water

Place the corn in a stone jar. Mix the lye and water and pour over the corn. Let soak for 15 hours or until outer layer comes off easily. Wash several times in cold water, rubbing to remove corn hulls. Cook, changing water 2 or 3 times, until tender. Pack in containers and freeze.

Eula Barker, Faubush, Kentucky

WILTED LETTUCE

4 slices bacon, chopped	2 green onions, chopped
1/4 c. vinegar	1 tsp. salt
2 tbsp. water	Dash of pepper
4 c. shredded lettuce	1 hard-cooked egg, chopped

Fry the bacon in a skillet until crisp. Add the vinegar and water and heat through. Mix the lettuce, onions, salt and pepper in a bowl. Add the hot bacon mixture and toss. Sprinkle with egg. 4 servings.

Mrs. Virginia Hines, Richmond, Virginia

GREEN PEPPER-CHEESE CASSEROLE

3 c. water	1 c. grated cheese
1 tsp. salt	8 saltine crackers, crumbled
1 c. elbow macaroni	3/4 c. milk
1 green pepper, sliced in rings	

Pour the water into a saucepan and bring to boiling point. Add the salt and macaroni and cook for about 15 minutes. Drain. Cook the green pepper in small amount of water for 5 minutes and drain. Arrange alternate layers of macaroni, green pepper, cheese and cracker crumbs in a casserole. Pour milk over top. Bake at 375 degrees for 30 to 35 minutes. 6 servings.

Mrs. Willis E. Wise, Pineville, Kentucky

BAKED CELERY

3 slices bacon, chopped	8 med. stalks celery, sliced
1 onion, thinly sliced	1 c. beef consomme
2 tbsp. finely chopped parsley	1/4 c. fine bread crumbs
1 sm. clove of garlic, crushed	3 tbsp. melted margarine

Place the bacon, onion, parsley, garlic and celery in a well-greased shallow baking dish and mix. Add the consomme and cover. Bake at 325 degrees for about 50 minutes or until celery is tender. Mix the bread crumbs and margarine and sprinkle over celery mixture. Bake for 10 minutes longer. 4 servings.

Julia Stevens, Columbia, South Carolina

SWEET AND SOUR CELERY AND ONIONS

1 stalk fresh Florida celery	1 tbsp. sugar
6 strips bacon	1/4 tsp. salt
1 c. sliced onion rings	1/4 tsp. white pepper
3 tbsp. cider vinegar	

Trim the celery and cut ribs into 1-inch pieces. Fry the bacon in a large skillet until crisp. Remove bacon and drain on paper towels. Pour off all except 3 tablespoons bacon fat. Add the celery and onion rings and saute for 5 minutes, stirring occasionally. Reduce heat and cover. Cook for 12 to 15 minutes or until vegetables are crisp-tender. Stir in the vinegar, sugar, salt and white pepper and heat through. Crumble the bacon over top and serve. 6 servings.

Sweet and Sour Celery and Onions (above)

FRITTER-FRIED OKRA

1 c. flour	2 eggs, well beaten
1 tsp. baking powder	1/3 c. milk
1/2 tsp. salt	5 c. thinly sliced okra

Sift the flour with baking powder and salt into a bowl. Add the eggs and milk and stir until smooth. Add the okra and mix. Drop by spoonfuls into deep, hot fat and fry until brown. 6-8 servings.

Mrs. Patsy Cooper, Goree, Texas

SOUTHERN OKRA

1 c. cut okra	1 tbsp. sugar
1 med. onion, chopped	1 tsp. flour
1 green pepper, chopped	1/2 tsp. salt
1/4 c. salad oil	1/2 tsp. pepper
1 c. canned tomatoes	

Cook the okra in boiling, salted water for 10 minutes, then drain. Brown the onion and green pepper in oil in a saucepan. Add the tomatoes and cook over low heat for 5 minutes. Add okra. Mix remaining ingredients and stir into okra mixture. Cook until vegetables are just tender, stirring occasionally. 4 servings.

Mrs. Joe H. Nickols, Dumas, Arkansas

BAKED ONIONS

6 lge. onions	1/2 c. boiling water
1/4 tsp. salt	3 tbsp. margarine
Pepper to taste	1/2 c. grated cheese
1 bouillon cube	

Place the onions in a baking dish and sprinkle with salt and pepper. Dissolve the bouillon cube in water and pour over onions. Add the margarine. Sprinkle cheese on top and cover. Bake at 350 degrees for 45 minutes. Uncover and bake for 15 minutes longer. 6 servings.

Mrs. Betty Feezers, Atlanta, Georgia

FRIED ONION RINGS

3/4 c. flour	1 egg, beaten
1/4 tsp. salt	3 lge. onions
1/2 c. milk	Oil
2 tbsp. vegetable oil	

Sift the flour and salt into a bowl. Add the milk, oil and egg and beat until smooth. Cut the onions into 1/4-inch thick slices and separate into rings. Dip each ring into batter and drain off excess batter over bowl. Heat 2 inches oil in a deep fryer to 375 degrees. Add the onion rings, several at a time, and fry for 2 to 3 minutes, turning occasionally. Drain on absorbent paper and sprinkle with additional salt. Leftover onion rings may be wrapped and frozen. Reheat in 350-degree oven for about 5 minutes. 4-5 servings.

Mr. D. J. Dear, Bay Springs, Mississippi

HERBED PEAS

1/2 c. sliced green onions	1/2 tsp. sugar
2 tbsp. margarine	1/2 tsp. salt
2 10-oz. packages frozen field	1/8 tsp. pepper
peas	1/4 tsp. basil
1/4 c. water	1 tbsp. parsley flakes

Saute the onions in margarine in a saucepan until soft. Add the peas and water and bring to a boil. Stir in remaining ingredients and cover. Simmer for 10 minutes. 4-6 servings.

Sister Mary Albertus, Tyler, Texas

HOPPING JOHN

1 c. dried black-eyed peas	3 c. cooked rice
1/4 lb. bacon or salt pork	Salt and pepper to taste
1 pod hot red pepper	

Place the peas in a saucepan and cover with water. Soak overnight. Add the bacon, hot pepper and enough water to cover and cook until peas are tender. Stir in the rice, salt and pepper. Pour into a casserole and cover. Bake in 350-degree oven until liquid is absorbed.

Mrs. O. C. Chesser, Bessemer, Alabama

VENETIAN RICE AND PEAS

4 slices bacon	2 c. chicken broth
1 sm. onion, minced	1 tsp. salt
3 tbsp. butter	Dash of pepper
1 10-oz. package frozen peas	1/4 c. grated Parmesan cheese
3/4 c. rice	

Cook the bacon in a heavy skillet until crisp. Drain and crumble. Saute the onion in butter in a saucepan until tender. Add the peas and cook for 5 minutes, stirring frequently. Add the rice and cook until coated with butter. Add the chicken broth, salt and pepper and pour into a casserole. Cover the casserole. Bake at 350 degrees until rice is done, stirring occasionally. Stir in the bacon and Parmesan cheese and serve. 6-8 servings.

Mrs. Tom W. Barron, Metairie, Louisiana

Caraway-Cheese Potatoes (below)

CARAWAY-CHEESE POTATOES

4 lge. potatoes, thinly sliced	1/2 c. water
1 8-oz. package shredded	1 tsp. salt
mozzarella cheese	1/4 tsp. pepper
2 eggs, beaten	1 tsp. caraway seed
1 2/3 c. evaporated milk	3 tbsp. butter

Preheat oven to 325 degrees. Place alternate layers of potatoes and cheese in a buttered 2-quart casserole. Combine the eggs, evaporated milk, water, salt, pepper and caraway seed and pour over cheese. Dot with butter. Bake for 1 hour or until potatoes are tender. 6 servings.

CHEESE-POTATO CASSEROLE

4 lge. potatoes, thinly sliced	2 slices American process cheese
Salt and pepper to taste	1/3 c. evaporated milk
1/2 stick margarine	

Cook the potatoes in boiling water for 15 minutes or until almost done and drain. Place in a 1 1/2-quart casserole and season with salt and pepper. Dot with margarine. Cut the cheese in 1/2-inch strips and place over the potatoes. Pour milk over the potatoes and cover casserole. Bake in a 400-degree oven for 15 minutes. Uncover and bake for 10 minutes longer or until lightly browned. 4 servings.

Mrs. Cecil S. Mizelle, Greenville, North Carolina

CRUNCHY POTATO BAKE

1/3 c. instant nonfat dry milk	1 tsp. salt
1/3 c. cold water	Dash of cayenne pepper
2 c. mashed potatoes	1 c. crushed corn flakes
1/4 c. finely chopped onion	1/2 c. grated cheese
1 egg, well beaten	3 tbsp. melted margarine

Mix the milk and water in a bowl until smooth. Add the potatoes, onion, egg, salt and cayenne pepper and beat until light and fluffy. Place in 1 1/2-quart casserole. Mix the corn flakes, cheese and margarine and spread over potato mixture. Bake at 375 degrees for 20 to 25 minutes. 6 servings.

Mrs. Ila McCarley, Bruce, Mississippi

DUCHESS POTATOES

3 c. hot mashed potatoes	1/8 tsp. pepper
3 tbsp. butter	3 eggs, separated
6 tbsp. milk	Melted butter
1 1/2 tsp. salt	

Mix the potatoes with butter, milk, salt, pepper and egg yolks, then fold in stiffly beaten egg whites. Place in a pastry bag and pipe onto a greased baking sheet in shape of heart. Brush with melted butter. Bake at 425 degrees for 5 minutes or until brown. 6-8 servings.

Mrs. Charlene Strickland, Danielsville, Georgia

Imaginative Idea for Leftovers
For scrumptious results, combine leftover mashed potatoes with your favorite recipe for refrigerator yeast rolls, bread, or pancake batter.

POTATO CASSEROLE

2 c. grated potatoes	1 tsp. salt
1/2 c. melted butter	1/4 tsp. paprika
2 eggs, beaten	1/2 c. milk
1 tsp. grated onion	1/2 c. grated sharp cheese

Preheat oven to 350 degrees. Place the potatoes, butter, eggs, onion, salt and paprika in a bowl and mix well. Place in a well-greased baking dish and pour milk over top. Bake for 40 minutes. Sprinkle with cheese and bake until cheese is melted and browned. 6 servings.

Mrs. George Siebenaler, Edinburg, Texas

BUTTERED RUTABAGAS

1 1/2 to 2 lb. rutabagas	1 tsp. salt
1 1/2 tsp. Worcestershire sauce	3 drops of hot sauce
1/4 tsp. onion powder	Margarine to taste
1/4 c. sugar	

Peel the rutabagas and cut into small cubes. Place in a saucepan and add Worcestershire sauce, onion powder, sugar, salt and hot sauce. Cover with water and bring to a boil. Reduce heat and simmer until rutabagas are tender and liquid has evaporated. Add the margarine and mash.

Mrs. Anne Sutphen Welch, Knoxville, Tennessee

ACAPULCO SPINACH CASSEROLE

2 pkg. frozen chopped spinach	3/4 tsp. garlic powder
4 tbsp. butter	3/4 tsp. celery salt
2 tbsp. chopped onion	1 tsp. Worcestershire sauce
2 tbsp. flour	2 or 3 drops of hot sauce
1/2 c. evaporated milk	1 6-oz. roll jalapeno cheese
1/2 tsp. pepper	

Cook the spinach according to package directions. Drain and reserve 1/2 cup liquid. Melt the butter in a saucepan over low heat. Add the onion and cook until soft. Add flour and stir well. Add the milk and reserved liquid slowly, stirring constantly and cook until smooth and thick. Add seasonings. Cut the cheese into small pieces and stir into sauce until melted. Add the spinach and mix well. Pour into a casserole. Bake at 350 degrees until heated through. The flavor is improved if casserole is refrigerated overnight before baking.

Mrs. Lewis F. Mitchell, McCool, Mississippi

LUNCHEON SPINACH

4 slices bacon	Dash of pepper
1 sm. onion, diced	1 c. milk
2 tbsp. flour	4 hard-cooked eggs, sliced
1/2 tsp. salt	1 pkg. frozen spinach

Cook the bacon in a skillet until crisp. Remove from skillet, drain and crumble. Pour off all except 2 tablespoons drippings from skillet. Add the onion and cook until tender. Add the flour, salt and pepper and mix well. Add milk and cook over medium heat, stirring constantly, until thickened. Add the bacon and eggs and mix. Cook the spinach according to package directions and drain. Place in a serving dish. Pour sauce over spinach. 4 servings.

Mrs. Evelyn Gose Owens, Albuquerque, New Mexico

SERBIAN SPINACH

1 pkg. frozen chopped spinach	1/4 lb. sharp cheese, cut
1 carton cottage cheese	in cubes
3 tbsp. flour	1/2 stick margarine, cut
3 eggs, lightly beaten	in pieces

Cook the spinach according to package directions and drain. Stir in remaining ingredients and place in a greased casserole. Bake at 350 degrees for 1 hour. 6 servings.

Mrs. Ruth Marie Skaggs, Morgantown, West Virginia

SPINACH TIMBALES

1 No. 2 1/2 can spinach	2 tbsp. butter or margarine
4 slices bacon, diced	2 tbsp. flour
3 eggs, slightly beaten	1 c. milk
Salt and pepper to taste	

Drain the spinach and place in a bowl. Fry the bacon in a skillet until crisp and add bacon and drippings to spinach. Add eggs and seasonings and mix well. Fill greased custard cups 2/3 full with spinach mixture. Bake at 350 degrees for 40 minutes. Melt the butter in a double boiler and blend in flour. Add the milk and blend well. Cook and stir until smooth and thick. Add salt and pepper and cover. Cook for about 8 minutes. Unmold spinach and serve with sauce.

June Houchins, Coleman, Texas

Celery Savings
Save the small celery stems and tops for soup and casserole recipes. Wash, chop, and store them in plastic containers in the freezer until needed.

SQUASH CROQUETTES

2 c. diced squash	1/2 tsp. salt
3 slices crisp bacon	1/8 tsp. pepper
1/4 c. chopped onion	1 egg, beaten
1/3 c. cracker meal	Bacon grease

Cook the squash in boiling water until tender. Drain and mash. Crumble the bacon and add to squash. Add the onion, cracker meal, salt, pepper and egg and mix well. Heat small amount of bacon grease in a skillet. Drop squash mixture by spoonfuls into bacon grease and fry until brown on both sides. Drain on paper towels. Cornmeal may be substituted for cracker meal.

Mrs. Darsy I. Hardy, Red Level, Alabama

Zucchini with Mock Hollandaise Sauce (below)

ZUCCHINI WITH MOCK HOLLANDAISE SAUCE

2 lb. zucchini	Dash of cayenne pepper
1 tsp. sugar	1 1/4 c. milk
1/2 c. butter	2 egg yolks, slightly beaten
3 tbsp. flour	2 tbsp. lemon juice
1/2 tsp. salt	

Wash the zucchini and cut lengthwise into quarters, sixths or eighths, depending on size. Cook in a small amount of boiling, salted water with sugar for 12 to 15 minutes or until just tender. Remove from heat and drain thoroughly. Add 1/4 cup butter and blend. Arrange on serving plate and keep warm. Melt remaining butter in a saucepan and stir in the flour, salt and cayenne pepper. Add the milk, and cook, stirring constantly, until thick and smooth. Reduce heat to low. Add small amount of the hot sauce to the egg yolks and blend. Stir back into remaining sauce. Add the lemon juice and blend. Serve at once with the zucchini.

CANDIED SUMMER SQUASH

2 med. yellow squash	2 tbsp. butter or margarine
1 c. dark corn syrup	Cinnamon to taste

Wash the squash and slice 1/2 inch thick. Arrange in a greased 1 1/2-quart baking dish. Pour syrup over squash and cover. Bake at 325 degrees for 35 to 45 minutes. Uncover and dot with butter. Sprinkle with cinnamon and bake for 10 minutes longer.

Vergie Kahln, Port Bolivar, Texas

SQUASH RING

6 c. sliced yellow squash	1/4 c. butter
1 med. onion, diced	1 tbsp. Worcestershire sauce
1/2 med. green pepper, diced	1/2 tsp. pepper
1 clove of garlic, diced	1/2 tsp. hot sauce
1 tsp. salt	1 c. bread crumbs
2 tbsp. sugar	3 eggs, well beaten
	1/2 c. milk

Cook the squash, onion, green pepper and garlic in 2 cups water in a saucepan until tender and drain well. Add remaining ingredients and mix. Place in a greased 1 1/2-quart ring mold and place in a pan of hot water. Bake at 350 degrees for 40 minutes. Unmold and fill center of ring with buttered green lima beans or English peas. Garnish with tiny pickled beets. 12 servings.

Mrs. Roy Wesley, Arlington, Virginia

GLAZED SWEET POTATOES AND APPLES

6 med. sweet potatoes	1/2 c. (packed) brown sugar
2 cooking apples, peeled	1 tbsp. water
1/4 c. butter	

Preheat oven to 350 degrees. Cook the sweet potatoes in jackets in a saucepan in enough water to cover until tender. Drain and cool. Peel and slice lengthwise in 1/2-inch slices. Cut the apples in thin slices. Place 1/2 of the sweet potatoes in a shallow 1 1/2-quart casserole. Cover with apples and top with remaining potatoes. Melt the butter in a small saucepan and stir in the sugar and water. Bring to a boil and pour over potatoes. Bake for about 45 minutes or until apples are tender, basting occasionally. 8-10 servings.

Freida Gates, Cardell, Oklahoma

Homemade Soup from the Freezer
Leftover vegetables and stock are tasty and nutritious ingredients for homemade soup. Keep a large plastic container in the freezer in which to store the leftovers that accumulate.

SWEET POTATO CROQUETTES

2 c. mashed sweet potatoes	2 eggs, slightly beaten
2 tbsp. melted margarine	3 tbsp. ground almonds (opt.)
1/2 tsp. salt	Finely sifted bread crumbs

Mix the sweet potatoes, margarine, salt, 1 egg and almonds and shape into balls. Roll in bread crumbs. Beat remaining egg and roll potato balls in egg. Roll again in crumbs. Fry in deep fat at 350-degrees for 3 minutes. 6 croquettes.

Mrs. A. T. Parker, Fayetteville, Arkansas

Country-Fried Tomatoes (below)

COUNTRY-FRIED TOMATOES

3 lge. firm tomatoes	Butter
Salt and pepper to taste	2 c. milk
Sugar	Finely minced parsley
Flour	

Peel the tomatoes and cut in half. Season cut sides with salt, pepper and small amount of sugar and dredge with flour. Melt 3 tablespoons butter in a heavy skillet. Add the tomatoes, cut side down, and cook over moderate heat until light brown. Turn and cook until heated through but not softened. Transfer to a heated platter and keep at serving temperature. Add enough butter to drippings in skillet to make 1/4 cup. Add 1/4 cup flour and blend. Add the milk and cook, stirring constantly, until smooth and thickened. Season with salt and pepper and spoon over tomatoes. Sprinkle with parsley and serve at once. 6 servings.

SCALLOPED TOMATOES WITH ONIONS

1 3 1/3-oz. can French-fried onions	Salt and pepper to taste
	Basil to taste
1 No. 303 can tomatoes	

Place 1/3 of the onions in a casserole and add 1/2 of the tomatoes. Repeat layers, ending with onions. Season with salt, pepper and basil. Bake at 400 degrees for 15 minutes or until bubbly. 3 servings.

Mary Masoney, Harrisonburg, Louisiana

MARY'S SCALLOPED TOMATOES

1/4 c. chopped onion	1 clove of garlic, minced
1 med. green pepper, chopped	3 tbsp. butter or margarine

1 c. toasted bread crumbs	1 tbsp. sugar
1 No. 2 1/2 can tomatoes	1 tsp. Worcestershire sauce
1 tsp. salt	

Saute the onion, green pepper and garlic in butter in a saucepan until tender. Blend remaining ingredients and add to onion mixture. Pour into a buttered casserole. Bake at 350 degrees for 20 minutes. 4-6 servings.

Mrs. Mary D. Tuggle, Asheville, North Carolina

WEIGHT WATCHERS' WINNER

1 1-lb. can tomatoes	2 tbsp. minced onion
2 lge. stalks celery, diced	1/4 tsp. salt
1/2 med. green pepper, diced	

Drain the tomatoes and reserve juice. Mix the reserved juice, celery, green pepper, onion and salt in a bowl and chill for several hours. Add the tomatoes and serve. 4 servings.

Mrs. J. C. Littlejohn, Tuttle, Oklahoma

TURNIP PUFF

1 tbsp. minced onion	1 tsp. salt
2 tbsp. butter or margarine	1 tbsp. sugar
2 tbsp. flour	1/8 tsp. pepper
3 c. mashed turnips	2 eggs, separated

Cook the onion in butter in a saucepan until tender but not brown. Add the flour and blend well. Add the turnips, salt, sugar, pepper and beaten egg yolks and stir well. Beat egg whites until stiff but not dry and fold into turnip mixture. Pour into a greased casserole. Bake at 375 degrees for 40 minutes. 6 servings.

Mrs. Shirley M. Shafer, Mobile, Alabama

SAUTEED FRESH TURNIP GREENS

1 lb. fresh tender turnip greens	1/4 tsp. pepper
2 strips bacon	1/2 tsp. sugar
1/3 c. chopped onion	2 tsp. lemon juice
1/3 c. minced green pepper	1 hard-cooked egg, sliced
1 tsp. salt	

Wash the turnip greens well and trim off coarse stems. Chop coarsely. Fry bacon in a skillet until crisp and remove from skillet. Crumble. Add the onion and green pepper to bacon fat in the skillet and saute until soft. Add the turnip greens and stir well. Cover tightly. Cook for about 10 minutes or until crisp-tender. Add the salt, pepper, sugar and lemon juice and toss lightly. Place in a serving dish and garnish with bacon and egg. 4 servings.

Zelma Langley, Vaughan, North Carolina

Mexican Dry Soup with Raisins (page 129)

frugal casseroles

Casseroles are famous as low-cost dishes which draw their flavor excitement from a blending of many flavors with just the right hint of seasoning — without the help of a lot of expensive ingredients. But they are much, much more than that. They are versatile, too. Casseroles provide a way to reuse leftovers . . . and at the same time introduce your family to a sparkling new taste treat. They are quick and easy to prepare — with careful planning, you can always have a casserole in your freezer for that busy day's supper or when unexpected company drops in.

With so much to offer, it's no wonder that casseroles are favorites with southern homemakers. Some of their finest recipes are those they have developed for casseroles . . . as a glance at the following pages will prove.

They transform beef into a Spanish-flavored treat in El Greco Casserole. Leftover turkey develops a new fillip of flavor in Bayou Turkey Dinner — a traditional favorite in southern homes. In Seven Seas Casserole these creative cooks blend fish flavors with subtle seasonings for an unforgettable dinner or luncheon dish.

For a change of pace, serve your family Best-Ever Liver Casserole or Tomato-Green Bean Casserole. These meals in a dish are real moneysavers — the kinds of casseroles you'll come to depend on for great flavor . . . at just pennies a serving!

123

Beef and Peach Paprika (below)

BEEF AND PEACH PAPRIKA

1 1-lb. 13-oz. can cling peach slices	1/2 tsp. pepper
1 1/2 lb. bottom round steak	2 tbsp. salad oil
1/4 c. flour	1 1-lb. can tomatoes
2 tsp. paprika	1 tsp. caraway seed
1 1/2 tsp. salt	Hot buttered noodles

Drain the peaches and reserve 1/2 cup syrup. Cut the steak into 2 x 1 x 1/2-inch strips. Combine the flour, 1 teaspoon paprika, 1/2 teaspoon salt and pepper. Heat the oil in a heavy skillet. Coat the steak with flour mixture and brown in oil. Reserve remaining flour mixture. Add reserved peach syrup, remaining paprika and salt, tomatoes and caraway seed and simmer, covered, for about 1 hour and 30 minutes or until tender. Mix reserved flour mixture with small amount of water and stir into steak mixture. Cook, stirring, until thickened. Add peach slices and heat through. Serve with noodles. 4-6 servings.

COUNTRY BEEF BAKE

2 lb. beef chuck	3 tsp. salt
1/4 c. flour	1/4 tsp. pepper
2 1/2 c. tomato juice	4 med. potatoes, thinly sliced
2 beef bouillon cubes	8 sm. onions, quartered
1 1/2 tbsp. corn syrup	1 acorn squash, split and seeded
1/4 c. finely chopped parsley	
2 cloves of garlic, minced	2 tbsp. butter or margarine

Trim fat from beef. Cut the beef in 1-inch cubes and coat with flour. Combine the tomato juice, bouillon cubes and corn syrup in a saucepan and heat to boiling point, stirring constantly to dissolve bouillon cubes. Combine the parsley, garlic, salt and pepper. Arrange half the potatoes in a 3-quart deep baking dish and sprinkle with some of the salt mixture. Top with half the onions and sprinkle with some of the salt mixture. Add half the beef. Repeat layers. Slice each squash half into 6 pieces and pare. Arrange over casserole and pour hot tomato juice mixture over squash. Dot with butter and cover. Bake at 350 degrees for 3 hours or until beef is tender. 6-8 servings.

Reginald Scott, Jr., Live Oak, Florida

EL GRECO CASSEROLE

2 tbsp. corn oil	1 tbsp. dark corn syrup
1 clove of garlic, minced	3 c. canned tomatoes
2 onions, sliced	1 tsp. salt
2 green peppers, cut in strips	1/2 tsp. pepper
2 lb. round steak, cut in cubes	2 to 3 tbsp. grape juice (opt.)
2 tbsp. cornstarch	1/2 c. sliced stuffed olives

Heat oil in a frying pan and add the garlic, onions and green peppers. Dredge the steak with cornstarch and add to frying pan. Cook, stirring frequently, until brown. Add syrup, tomatoes, salt, pepper and grape juice and place in a casserole. Cover. Bake at 350 degrees for 2 hours. Add the olives, then serve.

Mrs. Henry Kotzur, Edinburg, Texas

Bag-a-Chop
Small, reusable, plastic bags are the ideal freezer storage size for pork chops. Place small bags into a larger bag; seal and freeze. Individually wrapped chops are easily separated to reduce thawing time.

HOLIDAY CASSEROLE

2 lb. ground veal	1 tsp. salt
1 tsp. shortening	1/2 tsp. pepper
2 c. sliced celery	3 tbsp. lemon juice
1/2 c. chopped green pepper	1 c. mayonnaise
3 tbsp. grated onion	3/4 c. grated process cheese
1/2 c. sliced blanched almonds	3/4 c. crushed potato chips

Brown the veal in shortening in a skillet, then drain off excess fat. Add the celery, green pepper, onion, almonds, salt, pepper, lemon juice and mayonnaise and place in a greased 2-quart casserole. Cover with cheese and sprinkle potato chips around edge of casserole Bake at 350 degrees for 40 minutes. 6-8 servings.

Mrs. J. Jolly, Hale Center, Texas

SMOTHERED STEAK CASSEROLE

1 lb. round steak, cut in pieces	6 tbsp. shortening
Salt and pepper to taste	2 med. potatoes, sliced
Flour	1 lge. onion, sliced
	1 can refrigerator biscuits

Season the steak with salt and pepper and dredge with flour. Brown in shortening in a skillet. Place half the steak in a casserole. Add half the potatoes, then add half the onion. Add salt and pepper and repeat layers. Sprinkle 2 tablespoons flour over top and add enough water to cover all ingredients. Bake at 300 degrees for 1 hour and 30 minutes. Increase temperature to 375 degrees. Arrange biscuits on top of casserole and bake until biscuits are brown. 4 servings.

Mrs. Vernon Gustin, Dalhart, Texas

MEATBALL CASSEROLE

2 lb. ground beef	1 10 1/2-oz. can tomato soup
2 eggs, slightly beaten	1/2 c. water
1 c. soft bread crumbs	1 onion, chopped
1 c. applesauce	1 green pepper, chopped
1 tsp. salt	1 c. chopped carrots
1/4 tsp. pepper	1 c. chopped celery

Combine the beef, eggs, bread crumbs, applesauce, salt and pepper and shape into 3-inch balls. Brown in small amount of fat in a skillet, then place in 3-quart casserole. Blend the soup with water and stir in remaining ingredients. Pour over meatballs. Bake at 350 degrees for 1 hour or until meatballs are tender. 6-8 servings.

Mrs. Frank W. Cox, Glendale, Arizona

Tip for Leftovers

To prepare a nutritious, protein-rich, and tasty dinner, on short notice, combine leftover meats and cooked dried peas or beans.

CHEESEBURGER CASSEROLE

Butter	1 c. grated sharp Cheddar cheese
8 slices day-old bread, toasted	
1/2 lb. ground beef	1 egg, beaten
1/4 c. chopped onion	3/4 c. milk
2 tbsp. chopped celery	1/8 tsp. dry mustard
1 tbsp. prepared mustard	Dash of pepper
1 tsp. salt	Paprika

Preheat oven to 350 degrees. Butter both sides of the bread and cut diagonally. Mix the ground beef, onion, celery, prepared mustard and 1/2 teaspoon salt in a medium frying pan and cook over medium heat until beef is lightly browned. Place alternate layers of toast, beef mixture and cheese in a greased 9-inch square pan. Mix the egg, milk, dry mustard, pepper and remaining salt and pour over cheese. Sprinkle with paprika. Bake for 30 to 35 minutes. 4-6 servings.

Mattie Frederick, Turkey, North Carolina

MOUSSAKA

1/2 c. butter	1/2 tsp. cinnamon
4 c. thinly sliced potatoes	1/8 tsp. pepper
1 lb. ground beef	3 tbsp. flour
1 c. chopped onion	1/8 tsp. nutmeg
1 6-oz. can tomato paste	2 c. milk
1 c. water	2 eggs, slightly beaten
3 tsp. salt	1/2 c. shredded Parmesan cheese

Melt 1/4 cup butter in a large frypan. Add the potatoes and fry until lightly browned, turning frequently. Remove potatoes from frypan. Add 2 tablespoons butter to the frypan. Add the beef and onion and cook, stirring, until beef is crumbly. Add the tomato paste, water, 2 teaspoons salt, cinnamon and pepper and mix. Cook, stirring frequently, for about 15 minutes or until thickened. Melt remaining butter in a saucepan and blend in the flour, remaining salt and nutmeg. Add the milk and cook, stirring constantly, until thickened. Add a small amount of hot mixture to the eggs, stirring constantly. Return to saucepan and cook for 1 minute longer. Spread half the potatoes in a shallow 2-quart casserole and cover with beef mixture. Sprinkle with half the cheese and top with remaining potatoes. Cover with sauce and sprinkle with remaining cheese. Bake in 350-degree oven for 30 to 35 minutes or until lightly browned. Let stand for 10 minutes before serving. 6-8 servings.

Moussaka (above)

CASSEROLE DE BOEUF

1 lb. ground beef	1 can kidney beans (opt.)
1 1/4 c. elbow macaroni	Garlic salt to taste
2 lge. onions, chopped	Salt and pepper to taste
2 cans tomato soup	1 c. grated cheese
1/4 tsp. chili powder	

Brown the ground beef in a skillet. Cook the macaroni according to package directions and drain. Add the beef and remaining ingredients except 1/2 cup cheese. Place in a casserole and sprinkle with remaining cheese. Bake at 350 degrees for 20 minutes.

Mrs. Luther M. Hasty, West Point, Georgia

CHOW MEIN

1 1/4 lb. hamburger	1 No. 2 1/2 can tomatoes
Salt and pepper to taste	2 tbsp. Worcestershire sauce
1 8-oz. box sm. egg noodles	1 tsp. hot sauce
1/2 c. diced green pepper	1/2 tsp. seafood seasoning
1 c. diced onions	

Season the hamburger with salt and pepper and cook in a skillet until partially done. Cook the noodles according to package directions and drain. Place the hamburger in a casserole and cover with noodles. Add green pepper, onions, tomatoes, Worcestershire sauce, hot sauce and seafood seasoning. Bake at 350 degrees for 1 hour. 8 servings.

Mrs. Sallie M. Smith, Marion, South Carolina

CONFETTI CASSEROLE

1/2 lb. sliced bacon	Butter
4 tomatoes, sliced	1 green pepper or 1/2 onion,
Salt and pepper to taste	minced
1 1/4 tsp. sugar	1 can corn
1/2 c. bread crumbs	

Preheat oven to 425 degrees. Brown the bacon in a skillet and place in a 10-inch baking dish. Place 2 tomatoes over bacon and sprinkle with salt, pepper and 1 teaspoon sugar. Add half the crumbs and dot with butter. Sprinkle with green pepper. Add the corn and season with salt and remaining sugar. Dot with butter. Add remaining tomatoes and season with salt and pepper. Cover with remaining crumbs and dot with butter. Bake for 30 minutes. Fresh corn may be substituted for canned corn. 5-6 servings.

Mrs. Ramon E. Blevons, Virginia Beach, Virginia

HAM-A-LAY-A

1 can cream of mushroom soup	1 1/2 c. packaged precooked rice
1 1/4 c. water or milk	1 1/2 c. diced cooked ham
1/4 c. chopped onion	1 c. cooked green beans
1/2 tsp. salt	1 c. grated cheese (opt.)
Dash of pepper	Paprika to taste (opt.)

Combine the soup, water, onion, salt and pepper in a saucepan and mix well. Bring to a boil over medium heat, stirring occasionally. Pour half the soup mixture into a greased 1 1/2-quart casserole and add rice. Combine the ham and beans and place over rice. Top with remaining soup mixture and sprinkle with cheese and paprika. Cover. Bake at 375 degrees for 20 minutes. 4-6 servings.

Mrs. Hubert Roper, Decatur, Georgia

MEXICAN DRY SOUP WITH RAISINS

1 c. rice	3 tbsp. tomato paste
1 clove of garlic, minced	2/3 c. California seedless raisins
1/2 c. oil	2 canned green chilies, cut into
2 onions, cut in wedges	strips
1 lb. sliced smoked ham, cut in	2 1/4 c. boiling water
strips	Salt and pepper to taste

Brown the rice and garlic in oil in a skillet. Add the onions and ham and cook, stirring, until onions are transparent. Add remaining ingredients and cover. Simmer for about 30 minutes or until rice is tender.

Photograph for this recipe on page 122.

Chinese Vegetable Substitute

For an innovative and economical substitute in your next Chinese dish, use peeled, sliced radishes for the equivalent quantity of water chestnuts. Heat radishes in the chop suey or chow mein for the final 5 minutes, or until tender-crisp. Ten cents worth of radishes will replace one dollar's worth of water chestnuts.

PORK CHOP AND GREEN TOMATO CASSEROLE

6 pork chops	Salt
3 sm. onions, sliced	Pepper to taste
3 med. green tomatoes, sliced	1 tbsp. curry powder

Season the pork chops, onions and tomatoes with salt and pepper. Brown the pork chops in a skillet. Place alternate layers of chops, tomatoes and onions in a casserole and sprinkle with curry powder. Bake at 350 degrees for 1 hour. 6 servings.

Mrs. Sue Harrison, Keiser, Arkansas

Pork-Yam and Cherry Bake (below)

PORK-YAM AND CHERRY BAKE

6 med. Louisiana yams
6 loin pork chops, 1 in. thick
1/4 c. flour
1 1/2 tsp. salt
2 tbsp. salad oil
1 30-oz. can apricot halves

1 8-oz. jar red maraschino
   cherries
1 c. chicken broth
1/4 tsp. nutmeg
Dash of allspice
2 tbsp. lemon juice

Cook the yams, covered, in boiling, salted water for 30 to 45 minutes or until tender. Drain, peel and halve. Shake the pork chops in a paper bag with flour and 1/2 teaspoon salt until coated. Heat the oil in a large skillet over medium heat. Add the chops and cook for about 10 minutes on each side or until brown. Remove chops and set aside. Drain the syrup from apricots and cherries into the skillet. Stir in the broth, nutmeg, allspice, remaining salt and lemon juice. Return pork chops to skillet and cover. Simmer for about 35 minutes or until chops are tender. Remove chops to warm serving platter and keep warm. Add water to sauce, if necessary, for desired consistency. Add the yams, apricots and cherries to the skillet and cook just until heated through. Spoon yams, fruits and sauce over chops and serve. 6 servings.

ORANGE POTATOES WITH CHOPS

6 1/2-in. thick slices sweet
   potatoes
6 thin slices unpeeled orange
6 pork chops

1 tsp. salt
1/4 tsp. pepper
1/3 c. (packed) brown sugar

130

Place the potato slices in a greased oblong baking dish and cover with orange slices. Top with pork chops and season with salt and pepper. Sprinkle with brown sugar and cover. Bake at 350 degrees for 1 hour. Uncover and bake for 30 minutes longer. 4-6 servings.

Mrs. Roger S. Danner, Mexico Beach, Florida

PORK HASH IN CASSEROLE

2 med. onions, finely chopped	1 tsp. salt
Butter	Pepper to taste
1 c. diced cooked pork	1 1/2 c. cooked rice
1 c. tomato juice	1/2 tsp. Worcestershire sauce

Saute the onions in small amount of butter in a saucepan until tender. Add the pork, tomato juice, salt, pepper, rice and Worcestershire sauce and turn into a greased baking dish. Cover with boiling water. Bake at 300 degrees for 1 hour and 30 minutes.

Mrs. L. K. Halsey, Piney Creek, North Carolina

POTATO AND SAUSAGE CASSEROLE

4 potatoes, sliced	1 can mushroom soup
2 onions, sliced	1/3 c. water
1 lb. sausage, cooked	

Place half the potatoes in a greased casserole and add half the onions. Place half the sausage over onions and repeat layers. Mix the soup with water and pour over casserole. Bake at 300 degrees for 1 hour and 30 minutes. 4-6 servings.

Mrs. George Brooks, Meridian, Texas

SPARERIBS AND SAUERKRAUT

1 lge. can sauerkraut	1 lge. onion
1 lge. can tomatoes	2 lb. spareribs
2 tbsp. sesame seed	Salt and pepper

Combine the sauerkraut, tomatoes and sesame seed. Slice 1 slice from onion, separate into rings and reserve. Chop remaining onion and mix with sauerkraut mixture. Place in a baking dish. Cut the spareribs in serving pieces and season with salt and pepper. Place on sauerkraut mixture. Place reserved onion rings on spareribs and cover. Bake at 350 degrees for 2 hours. 5 servings.

Mrs. W. B. Skinner, Pensacola, Florida

CASSEROLE CHICKEN LOAF

4 c. diced cooked chicken	1 tbsp. (scant) sage
4 c. bread crumbs	1/2 tsp. salt
1/4 c. chopped pimento	4 well-beaten eggs
1/4 c. chopped onion	2 1/2 c. chicken broth
1/4 c. chopped celery	

Combine all ingredients except the eggs and broth in a bowl and mix well. Place in well-greased casserole. Mix the eggs and broth and pour over chicken mixture. Bake at 350 degrees for about 1 hour. 5 servings.

Ethel Wheat, Rogers, Arkansas

CHICKEN BREASTS AND POTATO CASSEROLE

4 to 6 med. potatoes, sliced	1/2 can cream of mushroom soup
2 lge. onions, sliced	3 chicken breasts, halved
Paprika to taste	Salt and pepper to taste
1/2 can cream of chicken soup	Butter

Place the potatoes in a heavily greased large casserole and add onions. Sprinkle with paprika and add the chicken soup and mushroom soup. Season the chicken with salt, pepper and paprika and place on soup. Dot with butter. Bake in 350-degree oven for 40 minutes. Cover with foil and bake for 50 minutes longer. 6 servings.

Mrs. Theo Moses, Lexington, Mississippi

CHICKEN-CHEESE MELTAWAY CASSEROLE

1 c. elbow macaroni	1/8 tsp. pepper
Butter or margarine	2 c. milk
1/4 c. finely chopped onion	1 1/2 c. diced cooked chicken
1/4 c. flour	4 slices cheese
1 tsp. salt	

Cook the macaroni according to package directions and drain. Melt small amount of butter in a saucepan. Add the onion and cook over low heat for 3 to 5 minutes. Stir in the flour, salt and pepper. Add milk gradually and cook until thickened, stirring constantly. Place half the macaroni in lightly greased 2-quart casserole and place half the chicken over macaroni. Repeat layers. Arrange cheese on top and pour sauce over casserole. Bake in 350-degree oven for 25 minutes. 4 servings.

Mrs. Lillie J. Smith, Pauline, South Carolina

CHICKEN-SWEET POTATO CASSEROLE

1 fryer, cut in serving pieces	2 med. sweet potatoes
Salt to taste	6 to 8 slices canned pineapple

1/2 c. pineapple juice   Butter
3 to 4 tsp. brown sugar   Cinnamon to taste

Season the chicken with salt and place in a large casserole. Cut the potatoes in 1/4-inch slices and place over chicken. Add the pineapple and pour pineapple juice over pineapple. Place 1/2 teaspoon brown sugar and a pat of butter in center of each pineapple slice and sprinkle with cinnamon. Cover with foil. Bake at 400 degrees for about 1 hour or until chicken is tender. 6 servings.

Imogene Huffman, Hattiesburg, Mississippi

BAYOU TURKEY DINNER

3 c. cooked rice   1/8 tsp. pepper
2 green peppers, coarsely   2 c. turkey gravy
   chopped   Dash of hot sauce
2 c. diced cooked turkey   2 tbsp. melted butter or
1 No. 2 can tomatoes   margarine
1 tsp. salt

Preheat oven to 350 degrees. Place alternate layers of the rice, green peppers, turkey and tomatoes in a greased 2 1/2-quart baking dish, seasoning each layer with salt and pepper. Mix the gravy, hot sauce and butter and pour over casserole. Bake for 30 minutes or until bubbly. 6 servings.

Mary Russell Cunningham, Evergreen, Alabama

Conscientious Buying
Separate the weekly grocery money. During a span of several weeks, average the family's food cost. Stay within this mean figure by compensating, when necessary, for extravagant spending one week with cautious spending the next. Additional reminder for economy's sake: buy only reputable brands.

INDIVIDUAL TURKEY CASSEROLES

1/2 c. flour   3/4 c. diced celery
1 tsp. salt   2 diced cooked carrots
1 c. cold turkey stock   2 1/2 c. diced cooked turkey
1 c. hot turkey stock   Minced onion to taste
3/4 c. cooked or canned peas   1 recipe pie pastry

Mix the flour and salt. Add the cold turkey stock slowly and mix until smooth. Add to hot turkey stock in a saucepan and cook until thickened, stirring constantly. Add peas and celery and cook for about 10 minutes. Remove from heat. Add the carrots, turkey and onion and mix lightly. Place in individual baking dishes and top with pastry. Bake at 425 degrees for 20 minutes.

Mrs. R. E. Williams, Maysville, Kentucky

TURKEY-CHEESE CASSEROLE

5 tbsp. flour	1 1/2 c. turkey broth
1 tsp. salt	1/2 c. grated cheese
1/4 tsp. onion salt	2 c. diced cooked turkey
1/4 c. melted butter	1/2 c. cooked peas
2 1/2 c. milk	1/2 c. chopped cooked carrots
1 1/3 c. packaged precooked rice	6 unbaked biscuits

Stir the flour, 1/2 teaspoon salt and onion salt into butter in top of a double boiler, then stir in milk. Cook over hot water, stirring occasionally, until thickened. Pour rice into a 2-quart baking dish. Combine the broth and remaining salt and pour over rice. Sprinkle with half the cheese. Mix the turkey, peas and carrots and place on cheese. Pour the white sauce over turkey mixture and sprinkle with remaining cheese. Bake at 375 degrees for 10 minutes. Place biscuits on top and bake for 10 minutes longer or until biscuits are brown. 6 servings.

Mrs. Grady Astrop, Bristol, Virginia

FISH AND GRITS LOAF

2 tbsp. chopped celery	2 tbsp. cream
2 tbsp. chopped onion	1 egg, beaten
1 tbsp. butter	1/2 tsp. salt
1 c. cooked grits	Pepper to taste
1 No. 2 can salmon	

Cook the celery and onion in butter in a saucepan until tender. Mix the grits with salmon and salmon liquid. Add the celery mixture and mix well. Add remaining ingredients and place in a greased baking dish. Bake at 300 degrees for 30 to 40 minutes.

Mrs. Charlotte Corley, South Miami, Florida

SAUCY SALMON

1 can cream of celery soup	1 1/4 c. crushed potato chips
1/2 c. milk	1 c. cooked green peas, drained
1 8-oz. can salmon	

Preheat oven to 375 degrees. Pour the soup into a 1-quart casserole. Add the milk and mix thoroughly. Drain and flake the salmon and add to the soup mixture. Add 1 cup potato chips and peas and stir well. Sprinkle with remaining potato chips. Bake for 25 minutes or until heated through.

Mrs. G. C. Thompson, Franklin, Tennessee

SEVEN SEAS CASSEROLE

1 can cream of celery soup
1 1/3 c. water
1/4 tsp. salt
1/4 c. finely chopped onion
Dash of pepper
1 7-oz. can tuna

1 1/3 c. packaged precooked
  rice
1 1/2 c. cooked peas
1/2 c. grated Cheddar cheese
Pimento strips (opt.)

Combine the soup, water, salt, onion and pepper in a saucepan and bring to a boil, stirring occasionally. Pour 1/2 of the mixture into greased 1 1/2-quart casserole. Drain and flake the tuna. Place alternate layers of rice, peas and tuna over soup mixture and cover with remaining soup mixture. Sprinkle with cheese and cover. Bake at 375 degrees for 20 to 25 minutes and garnish with pimento before serving. 4 servings.

Mrs. Evelyn Jones, Jackson, Tennessee

TUNA AND CHINESE NOODLES

1 5-oz. can chow mein
  noodles
1 can cream of mushroom soup
1/2 c. milk

1 c. chopped celery
1 7-oz. can white tuna,
  drained
1/2 c. cashew nuts

Place 1/2 of the noodles in a greased 1-quart casserole. Mix the soup, milk, celery, tuna and cashew nuts and pour over noodles. Sprinkle remaining noodles over top. Bake at 350 degrees for 30 minutes. 4 servings.

Mrs. Hubert W. Morgan, Memphis, Tennessee

Canned Soup Substitute
To bind casseroles, use leftover gravy in place of canned soup.

LEFTOVER LAMB

2 c. diced cooked lamb
1 c. lamb gravy
1/2 c. diced potatoes
1/2 med. onion, finely cut
1 green pepper, diced
1 can tomato sauce
1 sm. can pimento strips

1/2 tsp. paprika
1 tsp. Worcestershire sauce
1/2 tsp. salt
1/8 tsp. pepper
1 c. grated Romano cheese
Butter

Place the lamb in a baking dish and add the gravy. Cook the potatoes, onion and green pepper in boiling, salted water for about 10 minutes and drain. Mix the tomato sauce, pimento, paprika, Worcestershire sauce, salt and pepper and pour over the lamb mixture. Cover with cheese and dot with butter. Bake at 350 degrees for about 30 minutes or until brown. 6-8 servings.

Mrs. A. E. Soderholm, Henderson, North Carolina

TERESA'S CASSEROLE

6 lamb shoulder chops	1/2 tsp. pepper
1/3 c. melted butter or	1 c. canned chicken broth
margarine	2 parsley sprigs
2 c. finely chopped onions	4 whole cloves
1 clove of garlic, crushed	1 lb. potatoes
2 tsp. salt	

Preheat oven to 350 degrees. Brown the lamb chops on both sides in the butter in a large skillet and place in a 13 x 9 x 2-inch baking dish. Saute the onions and garlic in drippings in the skillet for 5 minutes or until tender and place over chops. Sprinkle with 1 teaspoon salt and 1/4 teaspoon pepper and add the chicken broth. Add the parsley sprigs and cloves and cover. Bake for 30 minutes. Pare and slice in potatoes and arrange over chops. Sprinkle with remaining salt and pepper and cover. Bake for 30 minutes. Uncover and bake for 30 minutes longer or until golden brown. 6 servings.

Teresa McMackin, Bruceton, Tennessee

MOUNTAINEER SQUIRREL

2 squirrels	1 1/2 tsp. salt
1 sm. onion	1/2 tsp. pepper
4 med. potatoes, cubed	Cornstarch
5 carrots, cut in 1-in. slices	Pastry for 2-crust pie
1 tsp. dried parsley flakes	

Place the squirrels and onion in a saucepan and cover with water. Bring to a boil and reduce heat. Simmer until squirrel meat is tender. Drain and reserve stock. Remove squirrel meat from bones. Place the potatoes, carrots, parsley and seasonings in a saucepan and cover with water. Cook until vegetables are almost done. Drain and reserve the liquid. Mix the reserved stock with reserved vegetable liquid in a saucepan and bring to a boil. Stir in enough cornstarch mixed with water for a medium-thick gravy. Line 8 x 12 x 2-inch baking dish with pie crust and pour the gravy, squirrel meat and vegetables into the crust. Cover with remaining pie crust. Bake at 375 degrees for 45 minutes or until crust is brown.

Mrs. Gertrude H. Willard, Langley AFB, Virginia

BEST-EVER LIVER CASSEROLE

1 1/2 lb. sliced beef liver	Salt and pepper to taste
5 potatoes, sliced	1 can cream of mushroom soup
5 onions, sliced	5 slices bacon

Brown the liver in small amount of fat in a skillet, then place in large baking dish. Place potatoes and onions over liver and sprinkle with salt and pepper. Pour soup over top and place bacon over soup. Bake at 350 degrees for 1 hour. 6 servings.

Mrs. V. H. Stevens, Searcy, Arkansas

BEEF AND PORK CASSEROLE

1 pkg. shell macaroni	1 lge. can cream-style corn
1 lb. ground beef	2 cans chicken-rice soup
1 lb. ground pork	Salt and pepper to taste
2 onions, chopped	1 c. bread crumbs
1 green pepper, chopped	

Cook the macaroni according to package directions until just tender. Brown the beef, pork, onions and green pepper in a skillet. Add the corn, soup and seasonings and mix well. Place in a greased baking dish and top with bread crumbs. Bake at 350 degrees for 45 minutes. 8 servings.

Mrs. William D. Smith, Georgetown, Kentucky

TURKEY-HAM CASSEROLE

1/4 lb. turkey	1 bay leaf
1/4 lb. ham	1 15-oz. can beefaroni
2 tbsp. butter	1 c. water
1 sm. onion, chopped	Dash of hot sauce
1/2 green pepper, chopped	6 frozen shrimp (opt.)
1/4 tsp. garlic powder	Chopped parsley

Cut the turkey in small pieces and cut the ham in strips. Brown the ham and turkey in butter in a skillet. Add the onion and green pepper and saute until tender. Add remaining ingredients except shrimp and parsley and cover. Simmer for 10 minutes. Add shrimp and cook for 3 minutes longer. Garnish with parsley and serve immediately. 6 servings.

Turkey-Ham Casserole (above)

137

BEEFY BEANS

1 lb. ground beef, crumbled	1/4 c. chili sauce
1/4 lb. bulk sausage, crumbled	1 1/2 tsp. salt
1 lge. onion, finely chopped	1/4 tsp. pepper
1/4 green pepper, chopped	1/4 c. wheat germ
1 can tomato soup	2 tbsp. grated Parmesan cheese
1 No. 2 can kidney beans	

Place the meats in a heavy skillet and cook for 2 minutes. Pour off some of the fat and add the onion and green pepper. Cook until brown. Stir in tomato soup, kidney beans, chili sauce and seasonings and bring to a boil. Pour into a 1 1/2-quart casserole and top with wheat germ and cheese. Bake at 350 degrees for 45 minutes. 6 servings.

Mrs. J. P. Berry, Barksdale AFB, Louisiana

CALIFORNIA OLIVE-BEAN BAKE

2 1-lb. 12-oz. cans baked beans	1 lb. firm ripe tomatoes
1 tbsp. vinegar	1 c. canned pitted California ripe
3 tbsp. prepared mustard	olives
2 tbsp. Worcestershire sauce	2 tbsp. chopped green onion
Dash of hot sauce	1/4 lb. shredded mozzarella cheese
1/2 tsp. salt	

Preheat oven to 400 degrees. Combine the beans, vinegar, mustard, Worcestershire sauce, hot sauce and salt in an 11 1/2 x 7 1/2 x 1 1/2-inch baking dish. Cut the tomatoes in 1/4-inch slices and arrange over beans. Bake for 20 minutes. Cut the olives into wedges and top baking dish with olives, onion and cheese. Broil until cheese melts. 10-12 servings.

California Olive-Bean Bake (above)

TOMATO-GREEN BEAN CASSEROLE

1 lb. fresh green beans, snapped	1/4 tsp. salt
2 tbsp. shortening	1/8 tsp. pepper
1/2 c. chopped onions	1 c. milk
2 tbsp. flour	2 c. grated sharp cheese
	2 ripe tomatoes, sliced

Cook the beans in boiling, salted water until tender. Drain and place in a greased 1 1/2-quart casserole. Melt the shortening in a saucepan. Add the onions and saute until golden. Stir in the flour, salt and pepper. Add milk gradually and cook, stirring constantly, until thickened. Add cheese and stir until melted. Pour 3/4 of the mixture over beans and cover with tomato slices. Add remaining sauce. Bake at 350 degrees until bubbly and golden brown. 4-6 servings.

Bonnie Kirk, Staffordsville, Virginia

SPINACH CASSEROLE

1 pkg. frozen chopped spinach	2 slices bread
1 tsp. sugar	3 tbsp. melted butter or
1 can mushroom soup	margarine
1 egg, slightly beaten	Dash of garlic salt
1 1/2 c. grated sharp cheese	

Cook the spinach with sugar in 1/2 cup water until tender and drain thoroughly. Add the soup, egg and cheese and mix well. Pour into a greased 1 1/2-quart casserole. Cube the bread and toss with butter and garlic salt. Place on spinach mixture. Bake at 350 degrees for 1 hour. 6 servings.

Mrs. J. McLean Murphy, Lowell, North Carolina

Two-for-One Casserole Idea
When preparing a casserole next, double the recipe and freeze one for future use. Fill a foil-lined ovenproof dish with the mixture and freeze until firm. The frozen block can be simply removed from the dish and wrapped for storage, freeing the ovenproof dish for use. Return the frozen block to the same dish for baking.

LIMA BEAN SCALLOP

1 1/2 c. dried lima beans	2 tbsp. butter
1 onion, chopped	1/4 c. bread crumbs
1 c. tomato soup	

Place the lima beans in a saucepan and cover with water. Soak overnight. Add the onion and bring to a boil. Cook over low heat until tender and drain. Add soup, 1/2 cup water and butter and pour into a greased casserole. Sprinkle with crumbs. Bake at 400 degrees for 30 minutes.

Mrs. W. G. Barr, Athens, Texas

SAVORY RICE

2 med. onions, finely chopped	1 tsp. dried marjoram
1 clove of garlic, chopped	1/2 tsp. dried thyme
3 tbsp. butter	1 tsp. dried chervil
1 c. converted rice	2 tsp. minced parsley
3 c. chicken broth	Salt to taste

Cook the onions and garlic in butter in a saucepan until tender. Add the rice and cook until lightly browned, stirring constantly. Add the broth and remaining ingredients and bring to a boil. Pour into a casserole and cover. Bake at 350 degrees for about 30 minutes or until rice is tender and liquid is absorbed. 4-6 servings.

Mrs. Vaughn Snow, Loudon, Tennessee

RICE POULEIN

1 c. rice	1/2 c. salad oil
1/2 lb. Cheddar cheese, grated	1 sm. onion, finely chopped
1/2 c. evaporated milk	Salt and pepper to taste
1/2 c. parsley flakes	

Cook the rice according to package directions. Add remaining ingredients and mix well. Place in a baking dish. Bake at 350 degrees for 45 minutes. 4 servings.

Mrs. Thomas A. Jones, Victoria, Texas

Soup Equivalents
For recipes requiring less than a full can of condensed soup, substitute a suitable amount of dry soup, which can be stored more successfully than canned soup.

CHEESE-SPAGHETTI CASSEROLE

1 8-oz. package spaghetti	1/2 c. chopped parsley
1 1/2 c. grated sharp cheese	1 sm. can pimento, chopped
3 eggs	1 med. onion, chopped
1/2 c. scalded milk	Salt and pepper to taste
1 c. soft bread crumbs	1 can mushroom soup
1/4 c. melted butter	

Cook the spaghetti in boiling, salted water until tender and drain. Place in a 4-quart casserole and sprinkle with 1 cup cheese. Beat eggs in a bowl and stir in the milk. Add the bread crumbs, butter, parsley, pimento, onion, salt and pepper and mix well. Pour over cheese and top with remaining cheese. Bake in 300-degree oven for 50 minutes. Heat the soup and pour over casserole. Bake for 10 minutes longer. 8 servings.

Mrs. M. B. Lamar, Atlanta, Georgia

Cheese and Noodle Casserole (below)

CHEESE AND NOODLE CASSEROLE

1 6 1/2-oz. package noodles	1/2 tsp. dry mustard
1/4 c. butter	2 1/2 c. milk
1/4 c. chopped green onions	1 c. shredded American cheese
1/4 c. flour	4 drops of hot sauce
1/4 tsp. salt	8 to 10 slices cottage ham roll,
1/2 tsp. paprika	cut in half

Cook the noodles according to package directions, then drain and rinse. Melt the butter in a saucepan. Add the onions and cook over low heat until soft but not brown. Blend in the flour, salt, paprika and mustard. Add the milk and cook, stirring constantly, until smooth and thickened. Stir in the cheese and hot sauce and blend well. Add the noodles. Pour into a 2-quart shallow casserole and arrange ham slices in rows on top of noodles mixture. Bake at 350 degrees for about 25 minutes or until bubbly. Sliced smoked butt or Canadian bacon may be substituted for ham roll. 6-8 servings.

MRS. HENDERSON'S CASSEROLE

1 med. package corn chips	1 can cream of chicken soup
2 c. grated cheese	1 sm. can evaporated milk
1 sm. can mild green peppers,	1 sm. onion, chopped
chopped	1 sm. can mushroom pieces

Place the corn chips in a greased 1 1/2-quart casserole. Mix 1 cup cheese with remaining ingredients and pour over corn chips. Place remaining cheese on top. Bake at 350 degrees for 30 minutes or until bubbly. 6-8 servings.

Mrs. Wayne Spies, Ft. Cobb, Oklahoma

penny-wise accents

To stretch a dish . . . to add bright notes of color and flavor to your table . . . to highlight any main course . . . accompaniments are a must. An accompaniment may be as simple as a small bowl of fluffy rice or as lavish as an elegant, highly-flavored sauce. Whatever you feature, your accompaniment should complement and enhance the flavor of your meal!

Southern homemakers like accompaniments because they offer a delightful way to round out a meal's nutritional values at low cost. Many times, leftover meats and vegetables accompanied by a brightly-colored tray of crisp relishes and pickles make a family-pleasing meal. Similarly, homemade jellies and preserves seem to add a note of special excitement whenever they appear on the table.

In this section, you'll find favorite southern recipes for every imaginable kind of accompaniment. Butters . . . catsups . . . chilies . . . jellies . . . preserves . . . pickles . . . relishes — these and more are represented by the finest recipes from southern homes. Serve your family home-made Tomato Catsup — there's a home-tested recipe waiting for you in the pages that follow. You'll also discover recipes for Cucumber Refresher, Glazed Orange Peel, Blackberry Jelly, Pear Mincemeat, and many more. All are family favorite recipes just waiting to make a hit with your family — and why not tonight!

APPLE BUTTER

8 c. applesauce	1/2 c. vinegar
6 c. sugar	1 sm. package cinnamon candies

Combine all ingredients in saucepan and cook, stirring frequently, for 30 minutes. Cool.

Hazel E. Schaad, Huntsville, Alabama

BAKED PEAR GARNISH

1 No. 2 can pears, drained	1 jar tart red jelly
1 box corn flakes, crushed	

Roll the pears in corn flakes and place on a cookie sheet. Bake at 350 degrees until corn flakes are brown and crisp. Place 1 teaspoon jelly in cavity of each pear and serve.

Clara Mae White, Brookhaven, Mississippi

CATSUP

1 gal. tomato juice	2 c. sugar
3 whole cloves	Dash of red pepper
1 lge. piece of cinnamon stick	1 tbsp. salt
1 c. vinegar	

Pour the tomato juice into a kettle and bring to a boil. Reduce heat and simmer until half the juice has evaporated. Tie the cloves and cinnamon in cheesecloth and add to tomato juice. Add remaining ingredients and cook to desired consistency. Remove cheese cloth and pour into sterilized jars. Seal.

Helen Ruth McElwee, Knoxville, Kentucky

Sweet Pickling

To prepare a batch of tasty sweet pickles, select less costly, whole dill pickles, slice into a jar, and combine with the following recipe: mix 1 cup dill pickle liquid, 2 cups sugar, 13 whole cloves, 1 tablespoon celery seed and 1 tablespoon mustard seed in a saucepan. Bring mixture to a boil and pour over dill pickles. Seal. In 2 days pickles will be ready to enjoy. Save the liquid for the next batch of homemade sweet pickles.

TOMATO CATSUP

20 lb. tomatoes, chopped	4 tbsp. paprika
6 med. onions, chopped	2 tsp. celery seed
4 med. sweet red peppers, chopped	1 tsp. whole allspice
2 c. vinegar	1 tsp. whole cloves
1 1/2 c. sugar	1 3-oz. package cinnamon sticks
2 tbsp. salt	

Combine the tomatoes, onions and red peppers in a kettle and cook, stirring occasionally, until tomatoes are soft. Press through a strainer. Place back in the kettle and add vinegar, sugar, salt and paprika. Tie remaining ingredients in cheesecloth and add to tomato mixture. Cook to desired consistency, then remove cheesecloth. Pour into sterilized bottles or jars and seal. 4 pints.

Beatrice Campbell, Leland, Mississippi

AVOCADO CREAM

2 ripe avocados	1 c. heavy cream, whipped
1/4 c. lime or lemon juice	Tomato wedges
Dash of hot sauce	Corn chips or tacos
Dash of paprika	

Halve the avocados lengthwise, twisting gently to separate halves. Insert a sharp knife directly into seeds and twist to lift out. Peel and quarter the avocados. Blend in electric blender with lime juice, hot sauce and paprika until smooth, then fold in the whipped cream. Place in a bowl. Serve with tomato wedges and corn chips or tacos. 3 cups.

Avocado Cream (above)

145

CELERY PINWHEELS

1 glass pimento cheese spread	1 bunch celery
Mayonnaise or salad dressing	

Soften the cheese and mix with enough mayonnaise to moisten. Separate the celery and fill each stalk with cheese mixture. Reassemble the bunch and tie with cord, if necessary. Wrap in waxed paper and chill thoroughly. Slice crosswise to serve.

Mrs. Arver L. Britt, Soperton, Georgia

CEREAL SCRAMBLE

1 lb. margarine	1 box crispy corn puff cereal
1/2 c. bacon drippings	1 box oat puff cereal
1 tsp. (heaping) garlic salt	1 box shredded rice cereal
Savory and celery salt to taste	2 cans peanuts
3 tbsp. Worcestershire sauce	1 sm. box pretzel sticks
1 tsp. hot sauce	

Melt the margarine and bacon drippings in a large Dutch oven. Add the garlic salt, savory, celery salt, Worcestershire sauce and hot sauce and mix well. Add the cereals, peanuts and pretzel sticks and mix well. Bake at 250 degrees for 1 hour, stirring frequently. Store in glass or tin containers in a cool place.

Mrs. Avery L. Cox, McAlester, Oklahoma

CHILI SAUCE

3 qt. chopped ripe tomatoes	1 tbsp. celery seed
3 c. chopped sweet red peppers	1/3 c. salt
3 c. chopped onions	2 c. vinegar
1 tbsp. broken stick cinnamon	3 c. sugar
1 tbsp. whole cloves	

Place the tomatoes in a colander and drain. Place in a kettle. Wash the red peppers and remove stems, seeds and membranes. Grind through fine blade of food chopper and add to tomatoes. Add the onions. Tie the cinnamon, cloves and celery seed in a cloth bag and add to tomato mixture. Add the salt and vinegar and bring to a boil. Reduce heat and simmer for 3 hours or until thick, stirring frequently. Add the sugar and cook for 30 minutes longer. Place in sterilized jars and seal. 5 pints.

Jean Cline, Morehead, Kentucky

CUCUMBER REFRESHER

2 med. cucumbers, thinly sliced	2 tbsp. vinegar
Salt	2 tbsp. sugar
1 med. onion, chopped fine	2 tbsp. salad dressing
	Pepper to taste

Mix cucumbers with 1 tablespoon salt and let stand for 5 minutes. Press with a plate, then drain. Repeat process 3 or 4 times and drain well. Combine remaining ingredients and mix well. Pour over cucumbers and stir. 4-6 servings.

Mildred Brown, Santa Fe, New Mexico

REFRIGERATED PICKLED CUCUMBERS

3 cucumbers, sliced thin	6 whole allspice
1 red onion, sliced thin	1 tbsp. chopped parsley
1 c. white vinegar	Salt and pepper to taste
1/4 c. sugar	

Place the cucumbers and onion in a bowl. Combine remaining ingredients and pour over cucumber mixture. Marinate in refrigerator for 24 hours. 6 servings.

Mrs. A. B. Crowe, Panama City, Florida

CRANBERRY-HAM AND NUT STUFFING

3/4 c. butter or margarine	1 13 3/4-oz. can chicken broth
1 c. chopped onion	1 1/2 c. minced smoked ham
1 c. chopped green pepper	1 c. chopped nuts
1 c. chopped celery	1 1/2 tsp. salt
1 1/2 c. fresh cranberries	1/2 tsp. pepper
10 c. stale Italian or French bread cubes	2 eggs, beaten

Heat the butter in a saucepan. Add the onion, green pepper and celery and cook until golden brown, stirring frequently. Pour into a bowl. Rinse and drain the cranberries and add to the onion mixture. Stir in remaining ingredients. Stuff turkey just before roasting. Sew or skewer opening and roast as usual. About 3 quarts.

Cranberry-Ham and Nut Stuffing (above)

147

CURRIED PEACH HALVES

1 16-oz. can cling peach halves, drained	2 tbsp. brown sugar
2 tbsp. melted butter or margarine	1/4 tsp. curry powder

Place the peach halves, cut side up, on rack in a baking pan and brush with butter. Mix the brown sugar and curry powder and sprinkle on peach halves. Bake at 300 degrees for 30 minutes. 6-8 servings.

Mrs. Vera D. Jacobs, Frankfort, Kentucky

GLAZED ORANGE PEEL

2 c. thick orange peel, cut in strips	2 c. sugar

Place the orange peel in a saucepan and cover with cold water. Bring to a boil and cook for 15 minutes. Drain well. Mix the sugar and 1 cup water in a saucepan and bring to a boil. Add the orange peel and reduce heat. Simmer for 25 minutes and drain. Roll in additional sugar and place on waxed paper until dry.

Photograph for this recipe on page 103.

PEACH JAM

4 c. chopped peaches	7 1/2 c. sugar
1/4 c. lemon juice	1/2 bottle liquid fruit pectin

Place the peaches in a large saucepan. Add the lemon juice and sugar and mix well. Place over high heat and bring to a boil. Boil for 1 minute, stirring constantly, then remove from heat. Stir in the pectin and skim off foam. Stir and skim for 5 minutes to cool slightly and to prevent peaches from floating. Ladle into glasses and cover with 1/8 inch hot paraffin. About 11 medium glasses.

Claude W. Dodd, Durant, Mississippi

Simple Cheese Spread

For a simple, yet appetizing cheese spread, process stale, dried cheese and several chunks of onion through a meat grinder.

BLACKBERRY JELLY

2 qt. ripe blackberries	1 box powdered fruit pectin
4 c. sugar	

Crush the blackberries. Place in cheesecloth or cloth bag and squeeze out juice. Measure 3 cups juice and pour into a large saucepan. Add the sugar and place over high heat. Add the fruit pectin and stir until mixture comes to a boil. Boil for 30 seconds, stirring constantly, then remove from heat. Skim and pour into sterilized jars. Seal and store in a cool, dry place.

Mrs. A. D. Allen, Magnolia, Texas

WINTER JAM

3 c. fresh cranberries	Juice and grated rind of 1 lemon
1 c. diced apples	1 c. canned crushed pineapple
1 1/2 c. water	3 c. sugar

Cook the cranberries and apples in the water in a kettle until tender. Press fruits and juices through a colander or strainer to remove skins. Add the lemon juice and rind, pineapple and sugar to pulp and return to the kettle. Bring to a boil over high heat and cook, stirring constantly, until thick and clear. Pour into sterilized jars and seal. Four 8-ounce jars.

Mrs. Mamie Rice, Kirshaw, South Carolina

PINK RUSSIAN DIP

1 pt. sour cream	2 tsp. angostura aromatic bitters
1 env. Russian salad dressing mix	

Place all ingredients in a bowl and blend well. May serve with cucumber strips, cherry tomatoes and olives. 2 cups.

Pink Russian Dip (above)

149

HOT PEPPER JELLY

3/4 c. ground bell peppers	1 1/2 c. white cider vinegar
1/4 c. ground hot peppers	1 bottle liquid fruit pectin
6 1/2 c. sugar	Green food coloring

Combine the peppers, sugar and vinegar in a saucepan and bring to a boil. Strain. Add pectin and enough food coloring for desired color. Pour into sterilized glasses and seal.

Noma A. Watkins, New Edinburg, Arkansas

ORANGE JELLY

2 c. lukewarm water	1/4 c. lemon juice
7 tbsp. powdered fruit pectin	4 1/2 c. sugar
1 sm. can frozen orange juice	

Pour the water into a 2-quart bowl and add the pectin slowly. Stir for 2 to 3 minutes. Let stand for 45 minutes. Place the orange juice in a saucepan and add the lemon juice and 2 1/4 cups sugar. Heat to lukewarm, stirring to dissolve sugar, then remove from heat. Add remaining sugar to pectin. Add to juice mixture and stir for 2 to 3 minutes. Pour into glasses and cool until set. Store in refrigerator. 8 glasses.

Mrs. Annie May Jones, Lueders, Texas

CHERRY TOMATOES MARINADE

1 c. vegetable oil	Salt and pepper to taste
1/4 c. wine vinegar	1 doz. cherry tomatoes, cut in
1 clove of garlic, crushed	half
1/2 tsp. oregano	

Mix the oil, vinegar, garlic, oregano, salt and pepper in a bowl. Add the tomatoes and chill for 2 hours. Drain the tomatoes. Marinade may be used as dressing for green salad.

Mrs. Guy D. Luke, Little Rock, Arkansas

MARINATED BEANS

1 c. dried lge. lima beans	1/4 c. wine vinegar
1/4 tsp. marjoram	1 tsp. sugar
1/4 c. chopped onion	Salt and pepper to taste
1/2 c. oil	

Cover the beans with water and soak for 6 hours or overnight. Cook in boiling water with marjoram until beans are tender, then drain. Mix remaining ingredients in a bowl. Add the beans and marinate until chilled. Drain beans and serve.

Mrs. J. L. Franks, Baltimore, Maryland

MARINATED BEETS

1 can tiny whole beets	1 tsp. salt
1/2 c. vinegar	1/4 c. (packed) brown sugar
1/4 c. salad oil	

Drain the beets and place in a 1-quart jar. Mix remaining ingredients and pour over beets. Cover and shake well. Refrigerate for 2 days, shaking jar frequently. Drain beets and serve.

Mrs. Guy Smithson, Marble Falls, Texas

CRANBERRY CHUTNEY

2 green apples	1/2 c. finely chopped preserved ginger
2 navel oranges	1/2 c. mixed candied fruit
4 c. fresh cranberries	6 whole cloves
1 c. (firmly packed) dark	6 whole allspice
brown sugar	1 tsp. salt
1 c. cider vinegar	1/4 tsp. mustard seed

Peel, core and dice the apples. Slice the oranges thin and dice. Combine all ingredients in a large saucepan and simmer for 15 minutes or until thickened, stirring toward end of cooking. Store in a sterilized jar in the refrigerator until served. May serve over pork chops. About 2 quarts.

Cranberry Pork Chops (page 54), Cranberry Chutney (above)

PEAR MINCEMEAT

18 c. ground pears	1 c. cider vinegar
2 pkg. seedless raisins	1 tbsp. cloves
1 orange, ground	1 tbsp. nutmeg
1 lemon, ground	1 tbsp. allspice
2 lb. sugar	

Combine all ingredients in a kettle and cook over low heat until pears are tender and mixture is thick, stirring occasionally. Pack in sterilized jars and seal. 10 pints.

Doris Strauss, Atlanta, Texas

BREAD AND BUTTER PICKLES

12 med. cucumbers	1/2 tsp. curry powder
5 med. onions	1 1/2 tsp. celery seed
1/4 c. salt	1 c. vinegar
1 c. sugar	1/2 c. water
1 1/2 tsp. mustard seed	

Wash the cucumbers and peel onions. Slice the cucumbers and onions 1/4 inch thick and separate the onions into rings. Place alternate layers of cucumbers and onions in a bowl, sprinkling salt on each layer. Let stand 2 to 3 hours, then drain. Combine remaining ingredients in a large saucepan and bring to a boil. Add cucumbers and onions and simmer for 10 minutes. Pack in hot sterilized jars and seal. 4 pints.

Mrs. Phil Ingle, Granite Falls, North Carolina

Homemade Chili Sauce
Blend an economical and practical homemade chili sauce for barbecuing or salad-making from the following ingredients: 1/2 teaspoon instant minced onion, 1/4 teaspoon chili powder, 1/8 teaspoon pepper, and 1 cup catsup.

CRISP PICKLES

5 lb. cucumbers	5 c. vinegar
1/2 c. lime	1/2 box pickling spices
7 c. sugar	

Slice the cucumbers and place in a stone crock or jars. Sprinkle with lime and add enough water to cover. Let set overnight. Rinse the cucumbers several times in cold water. Combine the sugar and vinegar in a large kettle. Tie the pickling spices in a bag and add to the sugar mixture. Add the cucumbers and cook until cucumbers are crystal clear. Pack into hot jars and seal.

Mrs. S. D. Scott, Marion, Virginia

OLD-FASHIONED PICKLED OKRA

4 lb. small tender okra	3/4 c. pickling salt
10 pods hot pepper	8 c. cider vinegar
10 cloves of garlic	1 c. water

Wash the okra and cut off tops, leaving short stems. Pack into 10 sterilized pint jars. Place 1 pod pepper and 1 clove of garlic in each jar. Combine the salt, vinegar and water in a saucepan and heat to boiling point. Pour over okra and seal jars. Let stand for several weeks before using.

Evelyn T. Haynes, Blytheville, Arkansas

SUNDIAL FRUIT PLATTER

2 Washington red Delicious apples	1 6-oz. package pasteurized
Lettuce or watercress	process Gruyere cheese
1 3-oz. triangle pkg. imported	2 sm. bananas
Roquefort cheese	2 Anjou, Bosc or Comice pears
1 8-oz. package old-fashioned	1/2 c. lemon juice
Cheddar cheese	8 slices American cheese

Place an apple on lettuce in center of a 12-inch plate or tray. Cut the Roquefort, Cheddar and Gruyere cheeses into 1/2-inch cubes. Insert picks in cheese cubes and spear into center of the apple. Peel the bananas and cut diagonally into 2-inch lengths. Core the remaining apple and pears and cut into thick slices. Dip all fruits in lemon juice to prevent discoloration. Arrange the banana lengths, spoke fashion, around center apple. Alternate the apple and pear slices in a circle around bananas. Cut the American cheese slices in half diagonally. Curve into half circles and place between grouped apple and pear slices. Serve with desired dressing.

Sundial Fruit Platter (above)

PICKLED PEACHES

20 to 24 sm. cling peaches   4 pieces of stick cinnamon
4 c. sugar   1 tbsp. whole cloves
2 c. vinegar

Peel the peaches. Mix the sugar and vinegar in a saucepan. Tie the cinnamon and cloves in a bag and add to sugar mixture. Bring to a boil and cook for 5 minutes. Drop peaches into syrup and simmer for about 15 minutes or until tender. Pack into hot sterilized jars. Strain syrup and pour over peaches in jars to within 1/2 inch of top. Seal the jars. 4 pints.

Mrs. Callie Neal, McMinnville, Tennessee

PICKLED WATERMELON RIND

4 qt. watermelon rind, cut in   1 tbsp. whole cloves
     2-in. squares   1 qt. vinegar
2 tbsp. salt   8 c. sugar
1/4 c. broken stick cinnamon

Remove peeling and pink portion from melon rind. Place in a saucepan and add enough boiling water to cover. Add the salt. Simmer until rind is tender, then drain thoroughly. Place in cold water and chill for at least 1 hour. Drain. Tie the cinnamon and cloves in a bag. Mix the vinegar and sugar in a kettle and bring to a boil. Add spice bag and watermelon rind and simmer until rind is clear and transparent. Remove spice bag. Pack the rind into hot sterilized jars. Cover with boiling syrup and seal. 4-5 pints.

Mrs. Paul T. Silvius, Milton, West Virginia

Fruitier Jellies

Leftover canned juices add a flavorful accent to homemade jellies. Reduce the amount of sugar, add 1 tablespoon of lemon juice, and continue preparation according to the directions on the fruit pectin package.

FIG PRESERVES

1 gal. figs   1 lemon, thinly sliced
6 c. sugar

Place the figs in a kettle and sprinkle with sugar. Let set for 4 hours or overnight. Bring to a boil. Add the lemon and reduce heat. Simmer until figs are tender and syrup is thick, stirring occasionally. Pack into hot, sterilized jars and seal. Turn jars upside down to cool to insure proper sealing. This recipe may also be used to preserve pears. 4 pints.

Mrs. Yvonne T. Napp, Butler, Alabama

TOMATO PRESERVES

7 lb. ripe tomatoes	**4 lemons, thinly sliced**
5 lb. sugar	**1/4 c. candied ginger**

Peel the tomatoes and chop. Place in a kettle. Add the sugar and lemons and cook over low heat until thick, stirring frequently. Cut the ginger in small slivers. Add to the tomato mixture and cook for 5 minutes longer. Pour into sterilized pint jars and seal. 6 pints.

Mildred H. Dodge, Macon, Georgia

A TRIO OF CHEESE DIPS

1 1/2 c. grated Cheddar cheese	**1/3 c. sour cream**
Mayonnaise	**1/8 tsp. salt**
3 tbsp. chopped pimento	**1/8 tsp. dillweed**
3/4 c. Cheddar cheese spread	**3 Washington red Delicious apples**
1 1/2 c. shredded Monterey Jack cheese	**2 tbsp. lemon juice**

Blend the Cheddar cheese, 1/2 cup mayonnaise and pimento in a bowl. Mix the Cheddar cheese spread and 3 tablespoons mayonnaise in another bowl. Blend the Monterey Jack cheese, sour cream, salt and dillweed in a separate bowl. Make diagonal cuts near top of each apple, each knife stroke at right angles to the preceding one, and cut just to center of apple. Lift off top, then hollow apple, using a melon ball cutter. Mix the lemon juice with 2 tablespoons water and dip apple cups in lemon mixture. Drain well. Tops may be dipped in lemon mixture and used as a decorative float in punch. Place each dip in an apple. Place the apples on a tray and garnish with mint.

A Trio of Cheese Dips (above)

155

CRANBERRY-ORANGE RELISH

4 c. fresh cranberries	2 c. sugar
2 unpeeled oranges, quartered	

Wash the cranberries and drain. Remove seeds from oranges. Grind the cranberries and oranges together and stir in the sugar. Place in a bowl and chill.

Mrs. John Beaulieu, Orlando, Florida

EGG RELISH

6 hard-cooked eggs, chopped	1/4 c. chopped onion
1 c. chopped celery	1/2 c. mayonnaise or salad
1/4 c. chopped parsley	dressing
1/4 c. chopped stuffed	1/2 tsp. salt
green olives	Dash of pepper

Place the eggs, celery, parsley, olives and onion in a mixing bowl. Fold in the mayonnaise, salt and pepper and cover. Chill. 2 1/2 cups.

Mrs. George R. Grindstaff, Old Fort, North Carolina

Cracked Egg Cure
If an eggshell cracks during cooking, add a small quantity of vinegar to the cooking water to prevent egg white seepage through the shell.

CIDER RELISH

1 env. unflavored gelatin	1/2 c. ground carrots
1 1/2 c. cider	1 c. chopped celery
1/4 c. sugar	1/2 c. ground cranberries

Soften the gelatin in 1/2 cup cider. Heat remaining cider in a saucepan but do not boil. Add the sugar and gelatin and stir until dissolved. Chill until slightly thickened. Add the carrots, celery and cranberries and mix. Pour into a 1-quart mold and chill until firm.

Mrs. Amy Pickens, Richmond, Virginia

RAISIN GARDEN RELISH

1/2 c. California seedless raisins	1 c. diced firm ripe tomato
1/4 c. (packed) brown sugar	1/2 c. finely chopped cucumber
1/4 c. garlic-flavored wine	2 tbsp. finely chopped green onion
vinegar	2 tbsp. finely chopped fresh mint
1 tsp. seasoned salt	1/4 c. finely chopped dill pickle
1 tbsp. cornstarch	

Combine the raisins, brown sugar, vinegar, salt and cornstarch in a saucepan and cook over moderate heat for about 5 minutes or until clear and thickened, stirring constantly. Cool. Chill remaining ingredients. Mix the raisin mixture with chilled ingredients just before serving. Relish stays fresh for 2 to 3 days if covered and stored in refrigerator. 2 cups.

Photograph for this recipe on page 142.

VEGETABLES VINAIGRETTE

1 1-lb. can artichoke hearts	Sugar
1 1-lb. can sliced beets	1 tsp. salt
1 1-lb. can whole kernel corn	1 sm. onion, sliced
2 8-oz. cans whole mushrooms	3 cucumbers
4 3/4 tsp. monosodium glutamate	1 1-lb. can ripe olives
Salad oil	1 red chili pepper
1 1/4 c. vinegar	3 sprigs of fresh dill
1/2 tsp. hot sauce	

Drain the canned vegetables and leave in cans. Reserve liquids except beet liquid to use in sauces, gravies and soups. Combine 4 teaspoons monosodium glutamate, 1 1/4 cups salad oil, 3/4 cup vinegar, hot sauce, 2 teaspoons sugar and salt in a bowl and beat until blended. Add the onion to beets. Pour the vinegar mixture over vegetables in cans and refrigerate for several hours or overnight. Cut the cucumbers into thin slices. Place in a bowl and sprinkle with 1/2 teaspoon monosodium glutamate. Combine remaining vinegar with 2 tablespoons sugar and 2 tablespoons water and pour over cucumbers. Chill. Drain the olives and leave in the can. Reserve liquid. Sprinkle olives with remaining monosodium glutamate and add the chili pepper and dill. Fill can 1/2 full with reserved liquid, then add 3 tablespoons salad oil. Fill to top with remaining reserved liquid. Chill for 8 hours or overnight. Drain the artichoke hearts, beets and onions, corn, mushrooms, cucumbers and olives and place in serving dish. Garnish the corn with diced pimento and green pepper. Garnish the cucumbers with fresh or dried dill.

Vegetables Vinaigrette (above)

Blueberry-Buttermilk Pancakes (page 168)

inexpensive breads

Breads have been called "the staff of life" — and with their high content of both vitamins and minerals, they well deserve that title. Southern homemakers appreciate both the nutritional value of bread and the many roles it plays in meal planning. So, they have developed many delicious recipes for all kinds of bread — quick and yeast loaves . . . muffins . . . biscuits . . . pancakes . . . waffles . . . rolls . . . and many more.

The very best of these home-baked bread recipes are now shared with you in the pages that follow by *Southern Living* homemakers. You'll discover how to prepare two traditionally favorite southern breads: Buttermilk Biscuits — a must at every meal from breakfast to dinner — and Crackling Bread, a corn bread beloved in homes from Virginia to Louisiana.

Traditional breads are not the only ones featured in this section. Smoothly flavorful Banana Bread . . . Crunchy-crusted French Bread . . . and all-time favorite Butter-horns are but three of the recipes you'll discover as you browse through these pages.

This is a section you'll come to depend upon again and again as you serve your appreciative family and friends homemade, flavorful, low-cost breads . . . based on recipes that have been favorites in southern homes for generations.

Delicious Orange Biscuits (below)

DELICIOUS ORANGE BISCUITS

2 c. sifted flour	Grated rind of 1 orange
1 tsp. soda	1 sq. unsweetened chocolate,
1 tsp. salt	grated
1/2 c. shortening	1 1/2 c. (about) buttermilk

Sift the flour, soda and salt together into a bowl. Cut in the shortening until mixture is consistency of cornmeal. Add the grated rind and chocolate and stir in enough buttermilk to make a soft dough. Place on a floured board and knead lightly. Roll out 1/2 inch thick and cut with a floured biscuit cutter. Place on an ungreased baking sheet. Bake at 475 degrees for about 15 minutes.

ALABAMA BISCUITS

2 1/2 c. all-purpose flour	6 tbsp. shortening
1/4 c. sugar	1 pkg. yeast
1 tsp. salt	1 c. lukewarm buttermilk
1 tsp. soda	Butter

Sift the flour, sugar, salt and soda together into a bowl and cut in the shortening. Dissolve the yeast in buttermilk, then stir into the flour mixture. Turn out onto a floured board and knead 30 times. Roll out 1/4 inch thick and cut with biscuit cutter. Butter tops and stack 2 biscuits together until all are stacked. Place on a baking sheet and let rise until doubled in bulk. Bake at 400 degrees until brown. 1 1/2 dozen.

Mrs. Janice Filty, Grayson, Kentucky

BAKING POWDER BISCUITS

2 c. flour	1/3 c. shortening
4 tsp. baking powder	2/3 c. milk
1 tsp. salt	

Sift dry ingredients together into a bowl and cut in shortening. Add the milk gradually and mix. Place on a floured board and knead. Roll out to 1/2 inch thickness and cut with a biscuit cutter. Place on a cookie sheet. Bake at 450 degrees for 12 to 15 minutes. 6 servings.

Mildred Richardson, White Mills, Kentucky

BUTTERMILK BISCUITS

2 c. flour	1 tsp. salt
1 tsp. baking powder	1/4 c. shortening
1/4 tsp. soda	2/3 c. buttermilk

Sift the flour with baking powder, soda and salt into a bowl and cut in the shortening. Stir in the buttermilk. Roll out on a floured surface and cut with a biscuit cutter. Place on a baking sheet. Bake at 450 degrees for 10 minutes.

Mrs. Vera Lineberger, Gastonia, North Carolina

Soups and Salads Perk-Up
Trim crusts from stale bread and save for bread crumbs. Cut the bread into 1/2-inch cubes for croutons. Bake at 325 degrees for 15 to 20 minutes, stirring occasionally, until golden brown.

CHEESE SWIRLS

1 c. sifted flour	2 tbsp. shortening
2 tsp. baking powder	1/3 c. milk
1/4 tsp. salt	1/2 c. shredded sharp cheese

Sift dry ingredients together into a bowl and cut in shortening until mixture is consistency of coarse crumbs. Add the milk all at once and stir just until mixed. Turn out on a lightly floured surface and knead for 30 seconds. Roll out to a rectangle 1/4 inch thick and sprinkle with cheese. Roll as for jelly roll and seal edge. Cut into 1/2-inch slices and place on a baking sheet. Bake at 425 degrees for 12 to 15 minutes.

Mrs. W. W. Clay, Atlanta, Georgia

CORNMEAL BISCUITS

1 1/2 c. self-rising flour   1/4 c. shortening
1/2 c. cornmeal   3/4 c. milk

Sift the flour with cornmeal into a bowl and cut in the shortening. Add the milk and mix. Roll out on a floured surface to 1/2-inch thickness. Cut with a biscuit cutter and place on an ungreased baking sheet. Bake at 450 degrees for 12 to 15 minutes or until brown. 1 dozen.

Mrs. Harry P. Tsumas, Statesville, North Carolina

Homemade Herb-Seasoned Bread Crumbs

Simple and economical to prepare, homemade, herb-seasoned bread crumbs, are another leftover specialty. Dry leftover bread slices in a 250-degree oven until crisp, but not brown. Break dried bread into a blender; blend at medium speed to form fine textured crumbs, or place bread in bag and crush with rolling pin. To season 1 cup of bread crumbs, add 1 tablespoon oregano, 1/2 teaspoon thyme, 1/2 teaspoon onion salt, and 1/8 teaspoon pepper. Store, covered, in a dry place, or freeze.

PINK BISCUITS

2 c. sifted flour   1/3 c. vegetable shortening
4 tsp. baking powder   3/4 c. tomato juice
1/2 tsp. salt

Sift flour, baking powder and salt together into a bowl and cut in shortening. Add the tomato juice gradually and mix. Roll out on lightly floured board and cut with a biscuit cutter. Place on a baking sheet. Bake at 450 degrees for 15 minutes.

Mrs. Russell O. Behrens, Apalachicola, Florida

EASY BREAD

1 1/4 c. self-rising cornmeal   1/4 c. oil
1 c. self-rising flour   1/2 c. milk
1 egg, beaten   1/2 c. hot water

Mix the cornmeal and flour in a bowl. Add the egg, oil, milk and hot water and beat thoroughly. Pour into a well-greased 8 x 12 x 1-inch pan. Bake at 400 degrees for 25 minutes. 8 servings.

Mrs. Helen W. Buffington, Lavonia, Georgia

CRISPY HUSH PUPPIES

1/2 c. sifted flour   1 tsp. salt
2 tsp. baking powder   3/4 c. milk
1 1/2 c. cornmeal   1 egg, well beaten
1 tbsp. sugar   1 sm. onion, chopped

Sift dry ingredients together into a bowl. Add the milk, egg and onion and mix well. Drop by teaspoonfuls into deep fat at 350 degrees and cook until brown. Drain and serve.

Mrs. J. M. Killingsworth, Mayfield, Oklahoma

CRACKLING BREAD

1 c. cornmeal	2 tsp. sugar
1/2 c. all-purpose flour	1 c. buttermilk
1 1/2 tsp. baking powder	1 egg
1/4 tsp. soda	1/2 c. cracklings
1 1/4 tsp. salt	

Sift the cornmeal with the flour, baking powder, soda, salt and sugar into a bowl. Add the buttermilk and egg and mix well. Stir in the cracklings. Pour into a well-greased skillet. Bake in 400-degree oven for about 30 minutes or until done.

Adell Biggs, Horse Cave, Kentucky

SAUSAGE-TOPPED CORN BREAD

6 to 8 link sausages	1 egg, beaten
1 c. sifted flour	1 c. milk
2 tsp. baking powder	1/3 c. corn oil
1 tsp. salt	1/2 c. chopped onions
3/4 c. cornmeal	

Cut three or four 1/8-inch deep diagonal slashes in sausages. Brown the sausages lightly in a frypan, drain and set aside. Sift the flour, baking powder, salt and cornmeal together into a bowl. Mix the egg, milk, corn oil and onions. Add to sifted ingredients and stir just until mixed. Pour into a greased 7 1/2 x 12 x 1 3/4-inch baking dish and arrange sausages, cut side up, on top of batter. Bake in 375-degree oven for 35 to 40 minutes or until lightly browned.

Sausage-Topped Corn Bread (above)

Blueberry Anadama Bread (below)

BLUEBERRY ANADAMA BREAD

1/4 c. yellow cornmeal	1 pkg. dry yeast
1 c. boiling water	1/4 c. lukewarm water
1 tsp. butter or margarine	3 c. (about) all-purpose flour
1/4 c. molasses	2 c. fresh or frozen dry-pack
1 egg, well beaten	blueberries

Stir the cornmeal into boiling water. Stir in the butter, molasses and egg and cool to lukewarm. Dissolve the yeast in lukewarm water and stir into cornmeal mixture. Beat in enough flour for a stiff dough and knead on a heavily floured board until smooth and elastic. Let rise in a warm place until doubled in bulk. Punch down and roll out on a floured board to a 10-inch square. Rinse and drain the blueberries. Sprinkle over dough and press into dough. Roll as for jelly roll. Tuck ends of roll under to seal and place the roll, seam side down, in a well-greased 9 x 5 x 3-inch loaf pan. Let rise in a warm place until doubled in bulk. Bake in a 375-degree oven for 45 to 50 minutes. Turn out and cool on a rack. Cool thoroughly before slicing. Spread with additional butter before serving.

BANANA BREAD

1 3/4 c. sifted flour	2/3 c. sugar
2 tsp. baking powder	2 eggs
1/4 tsp. soda	1 c. mashed ripe bananas
1/2 tsp. salt	1/2 c. chopped walnuts
1/3 c. shortening	

Sift flour, baking powder, soda and salt together. Cream the shortening in a mixing bowl. Add the sugar gradually and beat until light and fluffy. Add the eggs and beat well. Add flour mixture alternately with bananas, then stir in the walnuts. Turn into an 8 1/2 x 4 1/2 x 2 1/2-inch loaf pan. Bake in a 350-degree oven for 1 hour.

Mrs. Martha Wolfe, Tampa, Florida

CARROT BREAD

1 c. sugar	1 tsp. soda
2/3 c. salad oil	1 tsp. nutmeg
2 eggs, beaten	1 tsp. cinnamon
1/4 tsp. salt	1 1/2 c. flour
1 tsp. baking powder	2 c. grated carrots

Mix the sugar and oil in a bowl, then stir in the eggs. Sift the salt, baking powder, soda, spices and flour together and add to sugar mixture gradually. Stir in the carrots and place in a greased or waxed paper-lined loaf pan. Bake at 325 degrees for 1 hour.

Mrs. John C. Edge, Hurst, Texas

FAVORITE WHITE BREAD

3 pkg. yeast	3 tbsp. melted shortening
5 tbsp. sugar	2 tbsp. salt
1 c. instant nonfat dry milk	18 c. (about) flour

Dissolve the yeast in 1 cup warm water in a large bowl. Add the sugar, milk, shortening, salt and 5 cups lukewarm water and mix. Add the flour gradually and mix well. Let rise until doubled in bulk. Divide into 6 parts and knead each part well on a floured surface. Place in 6 greased loaf pans and grease top of dough. Cover with a large towel and let rise until doubled in bulk. Bake at 375 degrees for 40 minutes. Grease top of loaves and turn out on racks to cool.

Mrs. Douglas E. Holden, Dilley, Texas

From Batter to Bread
Don't hesitate to freeze leftover pancake and waffle batter to use in baking bread. Thaw batter and add to dough mixture.

FRENCH BREAD

1 pkg. yeast	1 tbsp. soft shortening
1 1/2 tsp. salt	4 c. flour
1 tbsp. sugar	Melted butter or margarine

Dissolve the yeast in 1/2 cup warm water. Dissolve the salt and sugar in 1 cup hot water in a bowl. Add shortening and yeast mixture and mix well. Add the flour, small amount at the time, and mix well. Let rest for 10 minutes, then cut through dough with a spoon. Repeat resting and cutting process 4 more times. Turn out onto a lightly floured surface and divide in half. Shape into 2 balls and let rest for 10 minutes. Roll each ball into a 12 x 9 rectangle, then roll firmly as for jelly roll, starting with the long side. Seal edges. Place on baking sheet and score top of each loaf 6 times diagonally. Cover with a towel and let stand for 1 hour and 30 minutes. Bake at 400 degrees for 30 to 35 minutes. Brush top with melted butter while hot.

Mrs. W. E. Fiorentini, Handsboro, Mississippi

OATMEAL BREAD

1 pkg. yeast	2 tsp. salt
1/4 c. lukewarm water	1/4 c. sugar
1/2 c. shortening	2 eggs, slightly beaten
2 c. oats	1/3 c. instant nonfat dry milk
2 1/2 c. boiling water	5 1/2 c. flour

Dissolve the yeast in lukewarm water. Mix the shortening, oats, boiling water, salt and sugar in a bowl and cool to lukewarm. Stir in the eggs, yeast and milk. Add the flour and mix well. Cover and let rise for 45 minutes. Knead lightly on a floured board and place in 2 loaf pans. Let rise for 45 minutes. Bake at 350 degrees for 40 minutes. Remove from pans and cool.

Elise Roach, Celina, Tennessee

POTATO BREAD

2 c. scalded milk	1 tbsp. sugar
1 pkg. dry yeast	1 1/2 tbsp. butter or margarine
1 c. cold mashed potatoes	6 c. (about) sifted flour
2 tsp. salt	

Pour the milk into a large bowl and cool to lukewarm. Sprinkle the yeast over milk and stir until dissolved. Blend in the potatoes, salt, sugar and butter. Add 4 cups flour gradually and mix well. Add enough remaining flour to make a stiff dough. Turn out onto a floured board and knead until smooth and elastic. Place in a greased bowl and turn to grease surface. Cover with a damp cloth and let rise in a warm place for about 1 hour or until doubled in bulk. Punch down and cover. Let rise for about 30 minutes or until doubled in bulk. Divide in half and place in 2 greased 7 1/2 x 4 1/2 x 3-inch loaf pans. Cover and let rise for about 45 minutes or until doubled in bulk. Bake in 350-degree oven for about 50 minutes. Remove from pans and cool on racks.

Mrs. Simon L. Blan, Clifton, Texas

Round Bread

Shape enough dough for 1 loaf bread into a ball and place in a greased, 2-pound coffee can. Allow dough to double in bulk or to reach the top of the can before proceeding with baking directions.

CORN MUFFINS

1 1/2 c. sifted flour	3/4 c. yellow cornmeal
3 tsp. baking powder	2 eggs, beaten
1 tsp. salt	1 c. milk
1/4 c. sugar	1/4 c. melted shortening

Sift flour, baking powder, salt, sugar together and add cornmeal. Place in a bowl. Add the eggs, milk and shortening and stir well. Pour into greased muffins cups. Bake at 425 degrees for 20 minutes.

Eunice Kelley, Walhalla, South Carolina

ORANGE MUFFINS

2 tsp. baking powder	1/4 c. melted margarine
1 1/2 c. sifted flour	1/4 c. milk
1/3 c. sugar	1/4 c. orange juice
1/4 tsp. salt	Grated rind of 1 orange
1 egg, well beaten	

Sift the baking powder, flour, sugar and salt together into a bowl. Combine the egg, margarine and milk. Make a well in the dry ingredients and pour in the egg mixture. Add the orange juice and grated rind and stir just until dry ingredients are moistened. Turn into greased muffin tins. Bake at 400 degrees for 30 minutes. 8-10 muffins.

Lynnie E. Oakes, Clermont, Florida

Greaseless Doughnuts
To prevent the greasy taste from lingering in doughnuts, add a small amount of vinegar to the deep fat while heating.

RAISIN-OATMEAL MUFFINS

3/4 c. sifted flour	1 c. dark seedless raisins
2 tsp. baking powder	2 eggs, slightly beaten
3/4 tsp. salt	1/2 c. milk
1/3 c. sugar	1/4 c. salad oil
1 c. rolled oats	

Sift the flour with baking powder, salt and sugar into a bowl. Stir in the oats and raisins. Combine the eggs, milk and oil. Add to dry ingredients and mix just until dry ingredients are moistened. Fill greased muffin cups 2/3 full. Bake in 400-degree oven for about 20 minutes. 12 muffins.

Mrs. Thad Saxton, Albany, Georgia

RICE MUFFINS

1 c. flour	1 egg
1 tbsp. sugar	2/3 c. milk
1/2 tsp. salt	1 c. cold cooked rice
1 1/2 tsp. baking powder	2 tbsp. melted shortening

Sift the flour, sugar, salt and baking powder together 3 times. Beat the egg thoroughly in a bowl and add the milk and rice. Stir in shortening. Add the flour mixture and stir just until dry ingredients are dampened. Spoon into greased muffin cups, filling 2/3 full. Bake at 425 degrees for 20 minutes or until browned. Serve hot. 8-10 muffins.

Mrs. George Pecsek, Virginia Beach, Virginia

CORNMEAL GRIDDLE CAKES

1 c. sifted flour	1 egg, well beaten
4 tsp. baking powder	2 c. milk
1 tsp. salt	2 tbsp. melted shortening
1 c. cornmeal	

Sift the flour, baking powder and salt together into a bowl. Add the cornmeal and mix well. Combine the egg and milk. Add to dry ingredients and mix well. Stir in shortening. Drop by spoonfuls onto a hot griddle and cook until brown, turning once.

Mrs. Frank Cress, Salisbury, North Carolina

BLUEBERRY-BUTTERMILK PANCAKES

2 c. fresh blueberries	3 tbsp. sugar
2 c. sifted flour	2 eggs, beaten
1/2 tsp. salt	2 c. buttermilk
1 tsp. baking powder	Melted butter

Wash the blueberries and drain in a colander. Sift 1 3/4 cups flour, salt, baking powder and sugar together. Mix the eggs, buttermilk and 2 tablespoons butter in a bowl. Add the sifted ingredients all at once. Toss the blueberries with remaining flour until coated and add to egg mixture. Stir just enough to moisten the flour and distribute the blueberries. Cook on a buttered griddle, using scant 1/4 cup batter for each pancake and turning when bubbles have formed on top side. Serve with desired syrup. Two cups frozen loose-packed blueberries, thawed and drained, may be substituted for fresh blueberries. 16-18 pancakes.

Photograph for this recipe on page 158.

Water Bagels (page 169)

BUTTERHORNS

1 c. scalded milk	1 pkg. dry yeast
1/2 c. shortening	2 eggs, beaten
1/2 c. sugar	4 1/2 to 5 c. flour
1 tsp. salt	Melted margarine

Combine the milk, shortening, sugar and salt in a bowl and cool to lukewarm. Add the yeast and stir well. Add the eggs and mix. Add the flour and mix until smooth. Knead lightly on a floured surface. Place in a greased bowl and cover. Let rise until doubled in bulk. Divide into thirds and roll each third on a lightly floured surface to a 9-inch circle. Brush with margarine and cut into 12 wedge-shaped pieces. Roll each wedge, starting with wide end, and place, point side down, on a greased baking sheet. Let rise until doubled in bulk. Bake at 375 degrees for 20 to 25 minutes.

Mrs. Joe DeJournette, Thurmond, North Carolina

Bargain Freezer Hint
When eggs are available at bargain prices, you may want to freeze them in quantity. Break carefully into plastic ice cube trays and freeze. When firm, transfer to plastic bags for storage.

WATER BAGELS

4 to 5 c. unsifted flour	1 1/2 c. hot tap water
3 tbsp. sugar	1 egg white, beaten
1 tbsp. salt	1 tbsp. cold water
1 pkg. dry yeast	

Mix 1 1/2 cups flour, sugar, salt and undissolved yeast thoroughly in a large bowl. Add tap water gradually and beat with electric mixer at medium speed for 2 minutes, scraping bowl occasionally. Add 1/2 cup flour and beat at high speed for 2 minutes, scraping bowl occasionally. Stir in enough additional flour to make a soft dough. Turn out onto a lightly floured board and knead for 8 to 10 minutes or until smooth and elastic. Place in an ungreased bowl and cover. Let rise in a warm place, free from draft, for 20 minutes. Dough will not be doubled in bulk. Punch down. Turn out onto a lightly floured board and roll into a 12 x 10-inch rectangle. Cut dough into twelve 1-inch strips and pinch ends of strips together to form circles. Place on ungreased baking sheets and cover. Let rise in warm place, free from draft, for 20 minutes. Dough will not be doubled in bulk. Fill a large, shallow pan with water to 1 3/4-inch depth and bring to a boil. Reduce heat. Add a few bagels at a time and simmer for 7 minutes. Remove from water and place on a towel to cool. Cool for 5 minutes, then place on ungreased baking sheets. Bake in a 375-degree oven for 10 minutes, then remove from oven. Mix the egg white and cold water and brush on bagels. Return to oven and bake for about 20 minutes longer or until done. Remove from baking sheets and cool on wire racks. 1 dozen.

CORNMEAL WAFFLES

1 c. flour	3/4 c. yellow cornmeal
1 tsp. salt	1 egg, beaten
2 1/2 tsp. baking powder	1 c. milk
2 tbsp. sugar	2 tbsp. melted shortening

Sift the dry ingredients together into a bowl. Mix the egg with milk and stir into dry ingredients. Beat well. Stir in the shortening and pour into hot waffle iron, small amount at a time. Bake until brown.

Mrs. J. L. Rabon, Lugoff, South Carolina

CRUNCHY COFFEE CAKE

2/3 c. (packed) brown sugar	1/2 tsp. salt
2 tbsp. butter or margarine	1 tsp. cinnamon
1/2 c. chopped nuts	1/4 tsp. nutmeg
Sifted flour	1/3 c. soft shortening
3/4 c. sugar	1 c. milk
2 tsp. baking powder	2 eggs

Combine the brown sugar, butter, nuts and 2 tablespoons flour in a bowl and chill. Sift 2 cups flour, sugar, baking powder, salt and spices together into a bowl. Add the shortening and milk and beat for 1 minute and 30 seconds. Add the eggs and beat for 1 minute and 30 seconds longer. Pour 1/2 of the mixture into a greased square baking dish and sprinkle with 1/2 of the chilled mixture. Cover with remaining spice mixture and sprinkle with remaining chilled mixture. Bake at 350 degrees for 35 to 40 minutes. 6-8 servings.

Mrs. Cleo H. Lemons, Sandy Ridge, North Carolina

STREUSEL-FILLED COFFEE CAKE

3/4 c. sugar	1 1/2 c. sifted flour
1/4 c. shortening	2 tsp. baking powder
1 egg	1/2 tsp. salt
1/2 c. milk	

Cream the sugar and shortening in a bowl. Add the egg and mix well. Stir in milk. Sift remaining ingredients together and stir into creamed mixture. Spread 1/2 of the batter in a greased and floured 9-inch square pan.

Streusel

1/2 c. (packed) brown sugar	2 tbsp. melted margarine
2 tbsp. flour	1/2 c. chopped nuts
2 tsp. cinnamon	

Mix all ingredients well and sprinkle batter with 1/2 of the Streusel mixture. Add remaining batter and sprinkle with remaining Streusel mixture. Bake at 375 degrees for 25 to 35 minutes.

Elgie Hurley, Randleman, North Carolina

BRAN DOUGHNUTS

1 tbsp. shortening	1 1/2 c. all-purpose flour
1/2 c. light corn syrup	2 tsp. baking powder
1 egg, well beaten	1 1/4 tsp. salt
1 1/2 c. whole bran cereal	1/4 c. milk

Cream the shortening and syrup in a bowl, then stir in the egg. Combine the cereal, flour, baking powder and salt and add to creamed mixture alternately with milk. Roll out on a floured surface 1/4 inch thick and cut with doughnut cutter. Fry in deep, hot fat until brown. Drain on absorbent paper.

Elouise McQuator, Woodville, Mississippi

CHERRY DOUGHNUTS

1 4-oz. jar red maraschino cherries, drained	1/2 tsp. nutmeg
1 13 3/4-oz. package hot roll mix	Vegetable shortening

Chop the cherries and drain on paper towels. Prepare hot roll mix according to package directions, adding nutmeg and cherries to yeast mixture before addition of flour mixture. Let rise until doubled in bulk. Roll out to 22 1/2 x 9-inch rectangle and cut into 4 1/2 x 1/2-inch strips. Twist strips and shape into cruller or doughnut shape. Let rise for about 35 minutes or until doubled in bulk. Fry 2 to 3 doughnuts at a time in deep shortening at 365 degrees for 2 to 3 minutes or until browned on both sides. Drain on paper towels and roll in sugar, if desired.

Cherry Doughnuts (above), Red Candy Apples (page 187)

171

Old-Fashioned Apple Shortcake (page 174)

bargain desserts

Desserts finish every meal with a very special flourish. Now, from the recipe files of great cooks throughout America's Southland, come favorite, money-saving dessert recipes — the memorable dishes these women serve their families and friends. Every recipe in this section was chosen not simply for eye-appeal or flavor goodness, but for low cost as well.

You'll delight in recipes like Gingerbread — serve it hot and fragrant to your family and watch their faces light up. For a not-too-rich dessert that's a hit with everyone, present Old-fashioned Jelly Roll at the end of your next meal. Dazzle the guests at your next luncheon or buffet party with an Orange Lemon Chess Pie. Based on an old English recipe — the "chess" originally was chest, for the place where this treat was stored — this pie is certain to win warm compliments for you and your cooking skills.

Favorite southern foods take on sweet tastes in dessert dishes, too, as in the recipe for Peach Princess. And Coffee Souffle is a light-as-air dessert that ends the richest meal with a just-right touch.

Every recipe you'll find in these pages has been proven successful in a southern home, a home where fine foods and excellent cooking are an old tradition. Introduce these desserts in your home — and end every meal with a delicious, low-cost flourish!

173

OLD-FASHIONED APPLE SHORTCAKE

6 med. Washington State Golden Delicious, Winesap or Jonathan apples	2 sticks whole cinnamon
	2 slices lemon
Sugar	Butter or margarine
2 c. water	Shortcake Biscuits
1/2 tsp. salt	1/4 tsp. vanilla
	1/2 c. heavy cream

Wash, pare, quarter and core the apples. Cut quarters in half lengthwise and set aside. Combine 1 cup sugar, water, salt, cinnamon and lemon slices in a 1 1/2-quart saucepan and mix well. Bring to boiling point. Add the apples and cover. Cook for 10 minutes or until apples are tender, stirring once or twice and being careful not to break apples. Turn off heat and let stand, covered, for 5 minutes. Remove apples from syrup carefully. Boil the syrup until thick, then return apples to syrup. Heap on the bottoms of buttered warm Shortcake Biscuits, spooning some of the syrup over apples. Top with remaining biscuit halves and apples. Add the vanilla and 1 tablespoon sugar to the cream and beat with a rotary or an electric beater until mixture stands in soft, stiff peaks. Spoon over shortcake.

Shortcake Biscuits

2 c. sifted flour	2 tbsp. sugar
1 tsp. salt	1/3 c. shortening
2 tsp. baking powder	2/3 c. (about) milk

Sift the flour, salt, baking powder and sugar together into a bowl. Cut in the shortening until mixture is consistency of crumbs. Stir in enough milk to make a soft dough, then knead for about 20 seconds on a lightly floured pastry board. Roll out to 1/2-inch thickness and cut with a 3-inch biscuit cutter. Place on an ungreased cookie sheet. Bake in 450-degree oven for 12 minutes. Split biscuits in half.

Photograph for this recipe on page 172.

BUTTERMILK POUND CAKE

3 c. sugar	3 c. flour
1 c. butter	1/2 tsp. salt
6 eggs, separated	1/4 tsp. soda
2 tsp. lemon extract	1 c. buttermilk

Blend the sugar and butter in a mixing bowl and add egg yolks, one at a time, blending well after each addition. Add the lemon extract. Sift dry ingredients together and add to sugar mixture alternately with buttermilk, beginning and ending with dry ingredients. Beat egg whites until stiff and fold into flour mixture carefully. Pour into tube pan. Bake at 350 degrees for 1 hour to 1 hour and 10 minutes. One teaspoon nutmeg may be substituted for lemon extract.

Jewell E. Smith, Coleman, Texas

GINGERBREAD

1/2 c. boiling water	1/2 tsp. salt
1/2 c. shortening	1/2 tsp. baking powder
1/2 c. sugar	1/2 tsp. soda
1/2 c. molasses	1/2 tsp. cinnamon
1 beaten egg	1/2 tsp. ginger
1 1/2 c. flour	

Pour the water over shortening in a bowl. Add the sugar, molasses and egg and mix well. Sift remaining ingredients together; add to the sugar mixture and beat until smooth. Pour into a waxed paper-lined 8-inch square pan. Bake at 350 degrees for about 35 minutes.

Sauce

1/2 c. sugar	1 c. water
1 tbsp. flour	2 tbsp. butter
Pinch of salt	2 tbsp. wine

Mix the sugar, flour and salt in a saucepan and stir in water. Bring to a boil and cook until thickened, stirring frequently. Add the butter and wine and stir until butter melts. Serve over Gingerbread.

Mrs. Paul Gowan, Mathews, Alabama

LEMON CHEESE CAKE

1/2 c. shortening	1/4 tsp. salt
2 c. sugar	1 c. milk
2 1/2 c. flour	4 egg whites, stiffly beaten
2 tsp. baking powder	

Cream the shortening and sugar in a mixing bowl. Sift the flour with baking powder and salt and add to the creamed mixture alternately with the milk. Fold in egg whites and reserve 2 tablespoons batter for filling. Pour remaining batter into 3 greased and floured cake pans. Bake at 350 degrees for 35 minutes.

Filling

Grated rind of 2 lemons	4 egg yolks
Juice of 2 lemons	1/2 c. milk
1 c. sugar	

Mix the grated rind, lemon juice, sugar, egg yolks, milk and reserved batter in a saucepan. Cook over low heat, stirring constantly, until thick, then cool. Spread between layers and on top and side of cake.

Mrs. J. A. Westbrook, Bascom, Florida

LIME PARTY CAKE

1 pkg. white cake mix	1 c. water
1 3-oz. package lime gelatin	1/2 c. shortening
4 eggs	1 tsp. vanilla

Place all ingredients in a mixing bowl and beat with mixer for 3 minutes or until well blended. Pour into a floured and greased 9 x 13-inch baking pan. Bake at 350 degrees for 30 to 35 minutes. Leave in pan.

Icing

1 1-lb. box powdered sugar	Grated rind of lemon
Juice of 2 lemons	

Mix all ingredients and pour on warm cake.

Mrs. R. D. Pundt, Floresville, Texas

OLD-FASHIONED JELLY ROLL

6 eggs, separated	1/4 tsp. salt
2 c. sugar	2 tsp. baking powder
5 tbsp. water	Jelly
2 c. flour	

Preheat oven to 350 degrees. Beat the egg yolks and sugar in a bowl until thick. Add water and mix well. Add the flour, salt and baking powder and mix until smooth. Fold in stiffly beaten egg whites. Pour into 3 greased 8 x 12-inch shallow baking pans. Bake until top springs back when lightly touched. Turn upside down onto damp towel immediately and spread with jelly. Roll from narrow end as for jelly roll and cool on rack. Slice and serve.

Mrs. W. A. Parker, Birmingham, Alabama

Nice and Easy
For a simple dessert topping, conveniently stored in either the refrigerator or freezer, mix 1 cup confectioners' sugar and 2 tablespoons frozen lemonade until smooth. Serve atop cakes, puddings, or custards.

PEACH MERINGUE

6 canned peach halves	1/4 c. powdered sugar
6 round cake slices	1/4 tsp. vanilla
2 egg whites	

Drain the peaches and place, round side up, on cake in a buttered pan. Beat the egg whites in a bowl until stiff, adding sugar and vanilla gradually. Cover peaches with meringue. Bake at 350 degrees for 10 to 15 minutes or until light brown and serve immediately.

Mrs. Maude Langdon, Chapmanville, West Virginia

QUICK STRAWBERRY-CREAM PARFAITS

1 c. milk
1 c. commercial sour cream
1/4 tsp. almond extract
1 3 3/4-oz. package vanilla-flavored instant pudding and pie filling

1 22-oz. can strawberry pie filling
Fresh strawberries (opt.)

Combine the milk, sour cream and almond extract in a large mixing bowl and mix well. Add pudding mix, then beat with an electric mixer 2 minutes or until creamy. Fill parfait glasses with alternate layers of pudding and strawberry pie filling and refrigerate. Garnish with strawberries, if desired. 6 servings.

Photograph for this recipe on page 2.

FRUIT ALASKA

1 No. 303 can fruit cocktail
3 tbsp. light rum
1 4-oz. package meringue mix

1/2 tsp. grated orange rind
6 individual sponge shortcakes
1 1/2 pt. ice cream

Drain the fruit cocktail well, drizzle with rum and chill thoroughly. Prepare meringue mix according to package directions and blend in the orange rind. Arrange the sponge shortcakes on a board and top with fruit cocktail. Place a firm scoop of ice cream on each and frost completely with meringue. Bake at 500 degrees for about 3 minutes or just until lightly browned. Serve at once. Six egg whites and 3/4 cup sugar may be substituted for the meringue mix. Beat the egg whites until soft peaks form, then beat until stiff, adding sugar gradually. 6 servings.

Fruit Alaska (above)

YAM BETTY

3/4 c. (firmly packed) dark brown sugar	3 lge. tart apples
	1/4 c. lemon juice
1/3 c. dark seedless raisins	1/4 c. water
1 tsp. salt	3/4 c. flour
1 tsp. cinnamon	1/2 c. butter
2 med. Louisiana yams, cooked	Whipped cream

Mix 1/4 cup sugar with the raisins, salt and cinnamon. Peel and slice the yams. Pare and slice 2 apples. Place alternate layers of yams and apples in an 8-inch square baking dish, sprinkling each layer with the raisin mixture. Combine 2 tablespoons lemon juice with water and pour over yam mixture. Blend the flour and remaining sugar in a bowl and cut in butter until mixture is crumbly. Sprinkle on top of baking dish. Bake in 350-degree oven for 30 minutes or until apples are tender. Slice remaining apple and cook in remaining butter and lemon juice in a saucepan until almost tender. Arrange on sugar mixture. Serve warm with whipped cream. One 16-ounce can yams, drained, may be substituted for cooked yams. 6 servings.

Photograph for this recipe on page 5.

SPICED LOUISIANA YAM PIE

1 1/2 c. mashed cooked Louisiana yams	1/4 tsp. ginger
	1/4 tsp. nutmeg
3 eggs, beaten	1/4 tsp. cloves
3/4 c. (firmly packed) dark brown sugar	3/4 tsp. salt
	1 lge. can evaporated milk
2 tsp. cinnamon	1 9-in. unbaked pie shell

Combine the yams, eggs, sugar, spices and salt in a bowl and beat until well blended. Stir in the undiluted evaporated milk. Pour into the pie shell. Bake in 375-degree oven for 55 minutes or until a knife inserted in center comes out clean. Canned yams may be substituted for fresh yams.

Photograph for this recipe on page 5.

CRUNCHY RAISIN PIE

3/4 c. malted cereal granules	1/4 c. cider vinegar
3/4 c. chopped raisins	3 tbsp. butter
1 1/2 c. (packed) brown sugar	1/2 c. chopped nuts (opt.)
2 1/4 c. hot water	Pastry for 2-crust pie

Combine all ingredients except pastry in a saucepan and cook for 10 minutes, stirring frequently. Cool. Roll out half the pastry on a floured surface and place in a pie pan. Trim edge. Pour raisin mixture into pastry in pie pan. Roll out remaining pastry and cut in strips. Place over pie in lattice fashion. Bake at 425 degrees for 15 minutes. Reduce temperature to 350 degrees and bake for 25 minutes longer.

Mrs. D. L. Sandefur, Temple, Texas

DEEP-DISH PEAR PIE

1 c. sifted all-purpose flour	1/4 c. grated Cheddar cheese
1/2 tsp. salt	2 to 3 tbsp. water
1/3 c. shortening	

Sift the flour and salt together into a bowl and cut in shortening until mixture resembles coarse cornmeal. Add the cheese and mix well. Stir in water, 1 tablespoon at a time, until pastry holds together, then chill.

Pear Filling

2 lb. pears	Dash of salt
1 tbsp. lemon juice	1/2 tsp. cinnamon
3 tbsp. flour	1/2 tsp. nutmeg
1 c. sugar	1 tbsp. butter or margarine

Peel the pears, cut in halves and remove cores. Arrange pear halves in a deep pie plate and sprinkle with lemon juice. Mix the flour, sugar, salt, cinnamon and nutmeg and sprinkle over pears. Dot with butter. Roll out pastry on a floured surface to a circle slightly larger than top of pie plate and cut several slits in center. Place over pears, crimping to edge of pie plate. Bake for 30 to 40 minutes at 350 degrees. Serve with cream.

Cathleen Adams, LaFayette, Alabama

Handy Freezer Pie Dough

A partially prepared pie dough can be mixed in volume and kept in the freezer, with only the addition of ice water necessary to moisten the frozen dough. Mix 3 pounds flour, 2 pounds shortening, 2 tablespoons sugar, and 2 tablespoons salt until mixture is of coarse consistency. Divide dough into six equal parts and store in freezer bags. Add the ice water and roll the dough out. Makes enough pie dough for 3 double-crust pies.

KENTUCKY PIE

4 eggs, separated	1 c. buttermilk
2 1/4 c. sugar	1/2 c. chopped nuts
Pinch of soda	1/2 tsp. cinnamon
2 tbsp. melted butter	1/2 tsp. allspice
1 c. raisins	2 unbaked pie crusts
1/2 tsp. cloves	

Beat the egg yolks in a bowl until lemon colored. Add 2 cups sugar, soda, butter, raisins, cloves, buttermilk, nuts, cinnamon and allspice and mix well. Pour into pie crusts. Bake at 350 degrees for 35 to 45 minutes. Beat the egg whites until stiff, adding remaining sugar gradually, and spread over pies. Bake for about 15 minutes longer or until lightly browned.

Mrs. Lawrence Jones, Bristol, Tennessee

Sour Cream-Lemon Pie (below)

SOUR CREAM-LEMON PIE

1 1/3 c. sifted flour	1 1/4 c. milk
1/8 tsp. salt	3 egg yolks, slightly beaten
3/4 c. margarine	1 tsp. grated lemon rind
2 tbsp. cold water	1/3 c. lemon juice
1 c. sugar	1 c. sour cream
1/4 c. cornstarch	Whipped cream (opt.)

Mix the flour and salt in a bowl. Cut in 1/2 cup margarine with pastry blender or 2 knives until mixture is consistency of fine crumbs. Sprinkle water over flour mixture and blend well. Press into firm ball. Flatten slightly and roll out to 12-inch circle on lightly floured surface. Fit loosely into one 9-inch pie pan and trim 1/2 inch beyond rim of pan. Fold under and flute edge. Prick thoroughly. Bake in 450-degree oven for 12 to 15 minutes or until golden brown. Do not prick shell if shell and filling are to be baked together. Mix the sugar and cornstarch in a 2-quart saucepan. Add the milk gradually and stir until smooth. Stir in the egg yolks, lemon rind and lemon juice. Add remaining margarine and cook over medium heat, stirring constantly, until mixture comes to boil and boils for 1 minute. Pour into a bowl and cover surface with waxed paper or plastic film. Chill, then fold in the sour cream. Turn into the baked pastry shell and chill. Serve with whipped cream.

OZARK PIE

1 egg	1/8 tsp. salt
3/4 c. sugar	1/2 c. chopped nuts
2 tbsp. flour	1/2 c. chopped apples
1 1/4 tsp. baking powder	1 tsp. vanilla

Beat the egg in a bowl for 1 minute. Add the sugar and beat until smooth. Sift the flour, baking powder and salt together and stir into the egg mixture. Add the nuts, apples and vanilla and mix well. Pour into a buttered 9-inch pie plate. Bake at 350 degrees for 35 minutes.

Mrs. John A. Murphy, Deerfield Beach, Florida

LEMON-ORANGE CHESS PIE

Grated rind of 1 lemon	3 eggs, slightly beaten
Juice of 1 lemon	2 tbsp. flour
Juice of 1 orange	1 1/2 c. sugar
1/2 stick butter, melted	1 unbaked pie crust

Place all ingredients except the pie crust in a mixing bowl and mix well. Pour into pie crust. Bake at 350 degrees until knife inserted in center comes out clean.

Mary Dietz, New Bern, North Carolina

Good to the Last Crumb
Store broken cookie bits and crumbs — the ideal ingredients for crumb crusts — in the refrigerator. As needed, roll crumbs to a fine texture.

CREAM PUFFS

1 c. all-purpose flour	1 c. water
1/4 tsp. salt	4 eggs
1/2 c. shortening	

Mix the flour and salt. Place the shortening and water in a saucepan and bring to a boil. Add the flour mixture and cook, stirring constantly, for about 1 minute or until mixture leaves side of pan and forms a ball. Remove from heat and cool. Add the eggs, one at a time, beating until smooth after each addition. Drop by tablespoonfuls onto ungreased baking sheet. Bake at 400 degrees for 40 to 45 minutes, then cool. Fill with sweetened whipped cream, custard, ice cream or sweetened fruit. 1 dozen.

Mrs. Lola Autrey, Shawnee, Oklahoma

SAND CRESCENTS

1 c. soft butter	2 c. flour
1 1/2 tsp. water	1/4 c. powdered sugar
2 tsp. vanilla	1 c. chopped nuts

Cream the butter in a bowl and stir in the water and vanilla. Add remaining ingredients and blend well. Shape into crescents and place on ungreased cookie sheet. Bake at 350 degrees for 30 minutes. Roll in additional powdered sugar while warm.

Mrs. B. R. Sparks, Hampstead, Texas

ORANGE COOKIES

3/4 c. shortening	1/2 c. sour milk
1 1/2 c. (packed) brown sugar	1/2 tsp. soda
3 tsp. grated orange rind	1/2 c. chopped nuts
2 eggs, beaten	1 tsp. vanilla
3 c. flour	1/3 c. orange juice
1 1/2 tsp. baking powder	1 c. confectioners' sugar
Pinch of salt	

Cream the shortening, brown sugar and 1 1/2 teaspoons grated rind in a mixing bowl. Add the eggs and mix well. Sift the flour with baking powder and salt. Mix sour milk with soda and add to creamed mixture alternately with flour mixture. Stir in the nuts and vanilla and drop from teaspoon onto a greased cookie sheet. Bake at 400 degrees until browned. Mix remaining grated rind with orange juice and confectioners' sugar and spread over cookies.

Mrs. Cleo Matthews, Davenport, Oklahoma

PEANUT BUTTER BROWNIES

2 eggs	1 tsp. vanilla
1 c. sugar	1 1/3 c. flour
1/2 c. (packed) brown sugar	1 tbsp. baking powder
1/4 c. peanut butter	1/2 tsp. salt
2 tbsp. margarine	1 c. chopped peanuts (opt.)

Combine the eggs, sugar, brown sugar, peanut butter, margarine and vanilla in a bowl and beat with mixer at medium speed until thoroughly blended. Add the flour, baking powder and salt and mix until smooth. Spread in greased 9-inch square pan and sprinkle with peanuts. Bake at 350 degrees for 30 minutes. Cut into squares while warm.

Carolyn Gorman, Arlington, Texas

Frozen Swirls
From leftover whipping cream, fashion whipped cream swirls and store in the freezer. Place swirls on a cookie sheet and freeze until firm. Carefully transfer to plastic wrap and reserve in freezer.

BLACKBERRY PUDDING

1 1/2 sticks butter, softened	3/4 tsp. soda
1 1/4 c. sugar	1 qt. fresh blackberries
1 egg, at room temperature	1 1-lb. box powdered sugar,
2 tsp. vanilla	sifted
2 c. flour, sifted	

Cream 1/2 stick butter and sugar in a mixing bowl. Add the egg and 1 teaspoon vanilla and mix well. Sift the flour and soda together and stir into the creamed mixture. Fold in blackberries and pour into a greased 9 x 9 x 3-inch pan. Bake at 350 degrees for 1 hour. Blend remaining butter with powdered sugar and remaining vanilla and serve with hot pudding. 8 servings.

Eurylee Yost Covington, Dade City, Florida

Moist Cakes Throughout Storage
If you are planning to store freshly baked cakes, beat 1/2 cup mayonnaise or salad dressing into the batter. The cake will remain tender and moist throughout storage, though the delicate flavor will not be harmed. Particularly recommended for prepared cake mixes.

CHOCOLATE-DATE PUDDING

1/4 c. shortening	2 1/2 tsp. baking powder
Salt	1 c. chopped dates
1 tsp. cinnamon	1/2 c. chopped nuts
Sugar	1/2 c. milk
2 oz. chocolate, melted	2 c. water
1 c. sifted flour	

Combine the shortening, 1/2 teaspoon salt, cinnamon and 1/4 cup sugar in a bowl and cream thoroughly. Add half the chocolate and blend. Sift flour and baking powder together. Mix 1/2 cup flour mixture with dates and nuts. Add remaining flour mixture to creamed mixture alternately with milk, blending well after each addition. Add the date mixture and blend. Combine 2/3 cup sugar, water, remaining chocolate and 1/8 teaspoon salt in a saucepan and bring to a boil. Pour into a casserole and drop date mixture by spoonfuls on hot syrup. Bake at 350 degrees for 45 minutes and serve warm or cold.

Mrs. Annie Ruth Cook, Bowdon, Georgia

PEACH PRINCESS

2 c. milk	1/4 tsp. nutmeg
4 c. bread cubes	Grated rind of 1 lemon
2 eggs, separated	Juice of 1 lemon
1/2 c. sugar	2 tbsp. melted butter
1/4 tsp. salt	1 can peaches, drained

Combine the milk, bread cubes, egg yolks, sugar, salt, nutmeg, lemon rind, lemon juice and butter in a bowl and mix well. Place in a greased baking dish and set dish in a pan of hot water. Bake at 350 degrees for 45 minutes. Beat the egg whites until stiff and spread on top of cooked pudding. Place peach slices on meringue and bake for 15 minutes longer.

Mrs. Dinnie Mizelle, Cofield, North Carolina

SOUTHERN-BAKED RICE PUDDING

4 c. cooked rice	1 c. sugar
2 c. milk	1 c. seedless raisins
2 eggs, beaten	1 tsp. nutmeg
2 tsp. vanilla	

Mix all ingredients and pour into a casserole. Sprinkle additional nutmeg on top and set casserole in pan of hot water. Bake at 350 degrees for 1 hour or until knife inserted in center comes out clean. Serve with whipped cream, if desired.

Eva Baker, Karnack, Texas

BAKED EGG FLAN WITH NUTMEG

6 eggs, well beaten	1 tsp. vanilla
1/4 c. sugar	4 c. milk, scalded
Dash of salt	Dash of nutmeg

Mix the eggs, sugar, salt and vanilla in a bowl and stir in milk slowly. Pour into a baking dish and sprinkle with nutmeg. Place in a pan of hot water. Bake at 350 degrees for 1 hour or until knife inserted in center comes out clean.

Mrs. Joe Shinault, Toone, Tennessee

Dashing Apple Pie
Be adventuresome with your favorite apple pie recipe: combine a dash of grated orange rind with sugar and sprinkle over apples; or, sprinkle grated cheese over pie pastry before rolling.

BUTTERMILK SHERBET

1 pt. buttermilk	1/4 tsp. salt
2/3 c. confectioners' sugar	1 1/2 c. crushed pineapple,
1 tsp. vanilla	drained

Mix all ingredients in a bowl. Pour into a refrigerator tray and freeze until partially frozen. Place in a bowl and beat well. Return to refrigerator tray and freeze until firm, stirring occasionally. 6 servings.

Mrs. Mike Snouffer, Jackson, Mississippi

MOCHA-FROSTED ICE CREAM ROLL

1/2 tsp. salt	Confectioners' sugar
4 eggs	1 qt. coffee ice cream
3/4 c. sugar	1/3 c. butter or margarine
1 tsp. vanilla	1 1/2 sq. unsweetened chocolate
3/4 c. pancake mix	Strong cold coffee

Preheat oven to 400 degrees. Combine salt and eggs in a mixing bowl and beat until thick and lemon colored. Add the sugar, small amount at a time, beating well after each addition. Add vanilla and pancake mix and stir until smooth. Spread in a greased and waxed paper-lined 10 x 15-inch jelly roll pan. Bake for 10 to 12 minutes. Loosen edges of cake and turn out onto a dry towel sprinkled with confectioners' sugar. Peel waxed paper from cake and roll cake in towel as for jelly roll. Let stand for 20 minutes. Unroll and spread ice cream over cake. Roll up and wrap in aluminum foil. Freeze for several hours. Cream the butter in a bowl. Add 1 1/2 cups confectioners' sugar slowly, beating constantly. Melt chocolate over hot water, then stir into butter mixture. Stir in 1 1/2 cups confectioners' sugar and enough coffee for spreading consistency and spread on frozen cake. 8 servings.

Mrs. Addie Davis, Salem, Kentucky

GINGER-PEACH ICE CREAM

1 15-oz. can sweetened condensed milk	1/3 c. thinly sliced preserved ginger
3/4 tsp. salt	1 c. whipping cream, whipped
1 tsp. vanilla	1 1-lb. 13-oz. can cling peach slices
1/4 tsp. almond extract	

Combine the milk, salt, vanilla, almond extract and ginger in a bowl and refrigerate until well chilled. Fold in the whipped cream and turn into freezer trays. Set control at lowest temperature and freeze until firm 1 inch from edge. Drain the peaches and crush 2 cups. Reserve remaining peaches for garnish. Turn partially frozen mixture into a chilled bowl and beat until smooth. Fold in crushed peaches and return to trays. Freeze until firm, stirring once or twice to distribute peaches and sliced ginger. Return temperature control to normal. Garnish servings of ice cream with reserved peaches. Three-fourths teaspoon powdered ginger may be substituted for preserved ginger. About 1 quart.

Ginger-Peach Ice Cream (above)

Angostura Mocha Chiffon (below)

ANGOSTURA MOCHA CHIFFON

2 tbsp. unflavored gelatin	2 9-oz. packages frozen whipped
3 c. water	topping, thawed
1/2 c. sugar	1 6-oz. package semisweet
1/4 c. instant coffee	chocolate pieces
1 tbsp. angostura aromatic bitters	1/2 c. coarsely chopped pecans

Soften the gelatin in 1 cup water in a saucepan. Add the sugar and coffee and stir over low heat until gelatin and sugar are dissolved. Add remaining water and angostura bitters and mix well. Chill until slightly thickened. Fold in 1 package whipped topping and place in a 9-inch springform pan. Chill until firm. Melt the chocolate pieces over hot water. Place a piece of foil over the bottom of a 9-inch layer pan. Spread melted chocolate evenly over the foil and chill until just firm. Cut into 8 wedges carefully with a knife dipped in boiling water, then chill the wedges. Remove gelatin mixture from pan and place on a serving platter. Spread remaining whipped topping over the top and push wedges of chocolate diagonally into topping all around cake. Sprinkle with pecans. Chill until ready to serve.

BUTTERSCOTCH-WALNUT WHIP

1 4-oz. package butterscotch	1/2 c. chopped walnuts
pudding mix	1 tsp. vanilla
1 tbsp. unflavored gelatin	1 tbsp. lemon juice
1 lge. can evaporated milk	1/4 c. (packed) brown sugar
1 c. water	

Combine the pudding mix, gelatin, 1 cup milk and water in a saucepan and cook until thick and smooth, stirring constantly. Add the walnuts, vanilla and lemon juice. Pour remaining milk into a refrigerator tray and freeze until ice crystals form around edge of tray. Place in a bowl and whip until stiff. Fold into pudding mixture and spoon into sherbet glasses. Sprinkle brown sugar over top and garnish with walnut halves. Refrigerate until chilled. 8-10 servings.

Lila Mae Jordon, Conway, South Carolina

COFFEE SOUFFLE

1 env. unflavored gelatin	2 tbsp. instant coffee
1/4 c. milk	1/4 tsp. salt
3 eggs, separated	6 tbsp. sugar
1 3/4 c. scalded milk	1/2 tsp. vanilla

Soften the gelatin in milk. Place the slightly beaten egg yolks in a saucepan and add milk slowly. Add the coffee, salt and 3 tablespoons sugar and cook over low heat, stirring constantly, until mixture coats a spoon. Add gelatin and stir until dissolved. Chill until thickened. Beat egg whites until foamy. Add remaining sugar gradually and beat until stiff. Fold in vanilla, then fold in gelatin mixture. Pour into mold rinsed with cold water and chill until firm. Garnish with whipped cream and shaved chocolate, if desired. 6 servings.

Mrs. Riley Franz, Ashland, Kentucky

CRUSTY PEACH COBBLER

1 No. 2 1/2 can sliced peaches	2 tsp. baking powder
1 1/2 tsp. lemon juice	1/4 tsp. salt
1/2 tsp. grated lemon rind	1/4 c. melted shortening
1/2 tsp. almond extract	1 egg, well beaten
1 c. flour	2 tbsp. sugar

Drain the peaches and reserve syrup. Arrange peaches in a greased 8-inch square pan. Combine 1/4 cup reserved syrup, lemon juice, grated rind and almond extract and pour over peaches. Bake at 350 degrees until heated through. Sift dry ingredients together into a bowl and stir in shortening, egg and 1/3 cup reserved peach syrup until dry ingredients are moistened. Spread over peach mixture and sprinkle with sugar. Bake for 30 minutes longer and serve with whipped cream or cream. 9 servings.

Mrs. W. B. Watt, Iva, South Carolina

RED CANDY APPLES

8 med. apples	1/2 c. water
1 c. sugar	1/2 c. red cinnamon candies
1 c. light corn syrup	

Wash and dry the apples and insert a wooden stick into stem end of each apple. Mix remaining ingredients in a saucepan and cook to hard-crack stage. Dip apples into syrup quickly and place on greased waxed paper. Cool.

Photograph for this recipe on page 171.

Clove and Cider-Simmered Apples (below), Apple Crisp (below)

CLOVE AND CIDER-SIMMERED APPLES

4 Washington State Jonathan or Winesap apples	3/4 c. water Juice of 1 orange
16 cloves	1 orange, thinly sliced
3/4 c. sugar	1 1/2 tbsp. lemon juice

Pare, core and quarter the apples and insert 1 clove in each apple quarter. Combine the sugar, water, orange juice, sliced orange and lemon juice in a saucepan and bring to a boil. Boil for 1 minute and lift out orange slices. Add the apple quarters to syrup and simmer for 5 to 10 minutes or until transluscent and tender but not mushy. Chill apples in syrup. Add orange slices to apples and serve. 4 servings.

APPLE CRISP

2 c. peeled, chopped apples	1/2 tsp. ground cinnamon
1/3 to 1/2 c. firmly packed brown sugar	1/2 tsp. ground nutmeg
1/4 c. all-purpose flour	3 tbsp. butter or margarine, softened

1/4 c. regular or quick-cooking
   oats
	Whipped cream or
	   ice cream (opt.)

Place the apples in two greased individual baking dishes. Combine remaining ingredients except whipped cream. Mix until crumbly and sprinkle over apples. Bake at 350 degrees for 30 minutes or until the apples are tender and topping is golden brown. Serve warm with whipped cream, if desired. 2 servings.

INDEX

PHOTOGRAPHY CREDITS: *United Fresh Fruit and Vegetable Association; Accent International; McIlhenny Company; Pet, Incorporated; Louisiana Yam Commission; National Macaroni Institute; Brussels Sprouts Marketing Program; National Kraut Packers Association; Apple Pantry: Washington State Apple Commission; Rice Council; Kellogg Company; Corning Glass Works; Turkey Information Service; Standard Brands Products: Fleischmann's Margarine, Fleischmann's Yeast; Ocean Spray Cranberries, Incorporated; Florida Fruit and Vegetable Association; Angostura-Wuppermann Corporation; North American Blueberry Council; Best Foods: A Division of Corn Products Company International; California Raisin Advisory Board; Green Giant Company; National Dairy Council; Spanish Green Olive Commission; National Cherry Growers and Industries Foundation; Procter and Gamble Company; American Dairy Association; Sunkist Growers; International Packers, Limited; National Association of Frozen Food Packers; Olive Administrative Committee; National Livestock and Meat Board; Cling Peach Advisory Board; Processed Apples Institute; California Prune Advisory Board; The R. T. French Company; Keith Thomas Company; Campbell Soup Company; Evaporated Milk Association; American Home Foods: Chef Boy-Ar-Dee.*

Printed in the United States of America.